JOURNEYS TO DOOR COUNTY

REVISED AND EXPANDED EDITION

TEXT BY MIKE LINK
PHOTOGRAPHY BY
CRAIG AND NADINE BLACKLOCK

VOYAGEUR PRESS

ACKNOWLEDGMENT

From the poetry of Robert Frost edited by Edward Connery Latham. Copyright 1916, 1923, © 1969 by Holt, Rinehart and Winston. Copyright 1936, 1944, 1951 by Robert Frost. Copyright © 1964 by Lesley Frost Ballantine. Reprinted by permission of Holt, Rinehart and Winston, Publishers.

This book is dedicated to my Great-Great-Grandmother Ogima′ bĭnĕsi′ Kwe, whom I never met, but think of often, for I know my feeling for the land comes from her.

— Mike Link

Printed in Hong Kong
90 91 92 93 94 10 9 8 7 6

ISBN 0-89658-049-0 (paper)
ISBN 0-89-658-048-2 (hardcover)

Published by Voyageur Press, Inc.
P.O. Box 338
123 North Second Street
Stillwater, MN 55082
In Minn 612-430-2210
Toll free 800-888-9653

Voyageur Press books are also available at discounts for bulk quantities for educational, fundraising, premium, or sales-promotion use. For details contact the marketing manager. Please write or call for our free catalog of natural history publications.

Contents

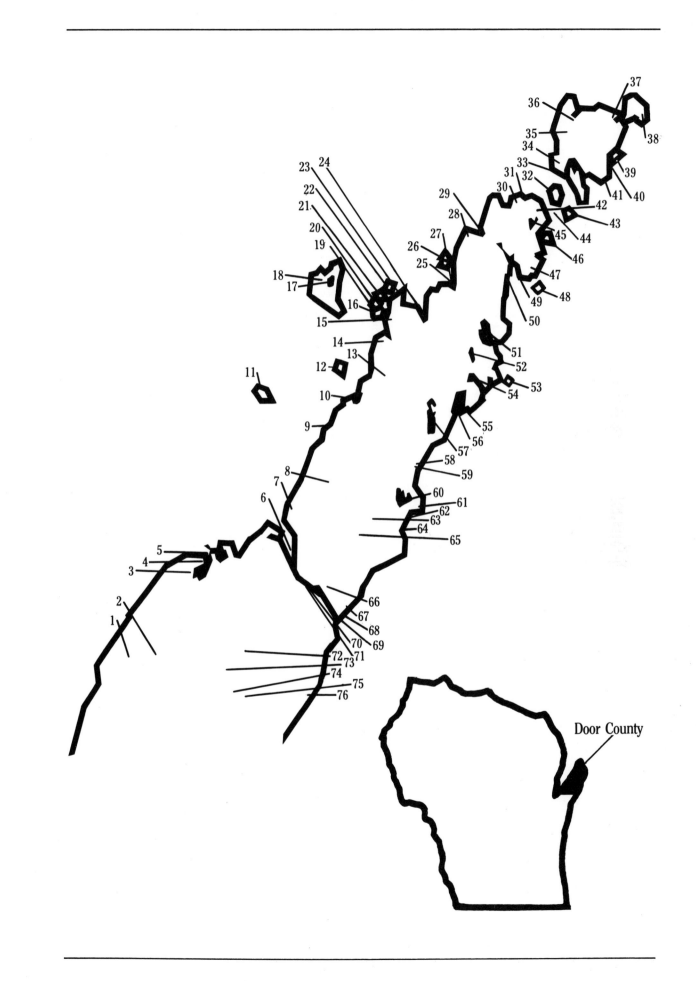

DOOR COUNTY

"HAVE YOU EVER THOUGHT ABOUT THE SIGNIFICANCE OF DOOR COUNTY?" JANE ASKED.
MY FIRST REACTION WAS: OF COURSE, WHY ELSE WOULD I WRITE A BOOK ABOUT IT? BUT THEN SHE ELABORATED FURTHER.

"If you said that you were going to Polk County, Pine County, or any other county, how many people outside of those areas would know where you were going? Mention Door County and millions of people nod and say, I know where that is. You don't even have to say what state it is in."

Only Sand County has the recognition of Door County, and that is just a fictitious county name referring to the setting of Aldo Leopold's essays. Among all of the borders, political units, and divisions, counties remain obscure, children of the state, memorized in fifth grade and then forgotten in the sixth.

Door County is a conundrum, an identity that encompasses people, towns, rural settings, landscape, environment, aesthetics, and escape. As a name, Door isn't the most exciting. It lacks the Native American charm of counties named Kewaunee, Sauk, or Winnebago; the historic character of the voyageur names of LaCrosse, Marquette, St. Croix, or Nicolet; and it doesn't roll off of the tongue like Manitowac or Trempeleau. It is simply a statement. Door County is a place, a destination.

It is probable that most people don't even associate the name with the channel, the bluff, and the shipwrecks that made Death's Door the focal point of the peninsula. It may be that more abstract associations are part of Door County's definition. In the twentieth century it has become a doorway to a disappearing charm, a route of escape for floods of people from Milwaukee, Chicago, and other urban areas.

Whatever the translation might be in historic or in modern terms, Door County is a symbol of what is the best about this region — Egg Harbor, Ephraim, Sister Bay, Baileys Harbor, the parks, the roads, the lake, the land, the people, and the wildlife.

Like ecology, Door County is the sum of all of these parts.

FLYING INTO GREEN BAY FROM DUE WEST, ONE VIEWS A LANDSCAPE THAT IS A MOSAIC OF FARMLANDS AND BLACKTOP, BROKEN BY THE CURVES AND MEANDERS OF WOODED STREAM VALLEYS. IT IS A

RETURNING

flattened work of glacial sculpture and deposition, a till plain, a ground moraine, and an assortment of sediments, gravels, boulders, and erratics. Forested lands seem artificially confined in rigid squareness. From the air it is difficult to assimilate subtle variations. Then, just as the plane begins to descend, there is a change in the forest, a distinct step that separates the layers of maple and pine.

The plane swings past the airport, and a great tongue of blue sweeps down from the north. As the plane turns, a marshland appears below, merging with industry and the bay. A sweep of land extends northeast and disappears into the mists of the lake as the plane turns our backs to the bay, and lands.

This is the beginning of a new journey to a land of old memories, to the tip of the peninsula called Door County. I am a little nervous. It has been three years since my last visit. This is an anniversary trip, eighteen years since my wife and I first came here together and twenty six years since my first journey. It has been said that a person should never revisit a place that has special memories, since time and change almost guarantee disappointment, and I wondered if the Door would fall short

of my expectations and the memories that I had poured into the first version of this book.

We drove north past the small remnant of marshland, over the bridge spanning the Fox River with its large ships and industry, past the campus of the University of Wisconsin, and into the rural landscape of the peninsula. The white gravel of the road's shoulders became my first Door County impression.

Lake Superior and its red and black volcanic rocks have been a part of many of my experiences. They extend down to my home, and the land that I walk regularly is red with their sediments. White rocks, limestone, dolomite, fossils, calcite, and calcareous depositions are from the sea, and here in Door County the gravel shoulders are rivers of Silurian deposition hundreds of thousands of years old.

The landscape glowed in autumn colors. Cranberry-colored dogwood leaves and bunches of yellow berries filled the band between a tan carpet of dried grasses and the green, yellow, and orange blaze of the forest. Maples radiated warmth, while the russet oaks gave the landscape strength and stability.

Reddish clay fields had been turned to the autumn sun, exposed to the October rains. The deposition of great glacial lakes was bared for spring planting and fall erosion. Most fields contained modern stone hedges, moved by calloused hands, horse, and tractor. Rock walls of blocky stone, punctuated with maples and sumac, drew lines across the fields, reaching from roadway to woods. I knew again why I loved this landscape.

Door County still has the charm of raw wood and stone structures. It is a rare and precious testimony to the potential harmony between man and nature, the best of rural landscape. It is also a precarious land, with limts for growth and development, with fragile charms that suffer when crowded.

It is a canvas of creative expression, with a football field framed in maples and white pines; a solitary sailboat anchored in a sea of white floats and waves, like the last leaf fluttering in a November wind; a tugboat drooping ropes and tires from its low-slung deck; and a palette of colors flowing from the valley walls, cascading through Juddville and on toward Lake Michigan.

There were some disappointments on this visit, especially the threat of headlong development, but there was still satisfaction. Memories flowed freely as we passed through each town and past the farms, memories bathed in pleasantness by time.

How many ways do people see Door County? How many different perspectives are there, and which ones are correct? Who can see what I see and feel what I feel? This is the constant problem of the author, the difficulty in communication.

Descartes, a philosopher of an earlier age, wrote, "I think, therefore I am." With that he began an entire school of philosophy. It seems now that we each see and experience in our own way. I only hope that my insights might help you to find a personal satisfaction and a concern for Door County.

GREEN BAY

THE NAME GREEN BAY HAS BECOME SO LINKED WITH THE NATIONAL FOOTBALL LEAGUE THAT ONLY A FEW PEOPLE ASSOCIATE IT WITH A CITY, AND FEWER STILL THINK OF IT AS A LARGE BODY OF WATER. GREEN BAY IS ALMOST A GREAT LAKE IN ITSELF, A SIAMESE TWIN OF LAKE MICHIGAN, SURROUNDED BY DOOR COUNTY PENINSULA, GARDEN PENINSULA, A STRING OF ISLANDS ON ONE SIDE, AND THE UPPER Peninsula of Michigan on the other.

Green Bay is a sailor's paradise, large enough for a good week's sail, yet small enough to have havens from the storms. The islands and peninsulas on the east present an armor of cliffs broken by sheltered bays and channels, while the west shore slopes gently beneath the blue waters.

Door County offers an intriguing vista from the water. Mural escarpments of limestone are framed by cedars, pines, and hardwoods. Islands break up the open waters of the bay and are temptresses to the billowing sail, offering perched sanctuaries and sandy beaches that call out like sirens to the sailor.

But temptation is not to be taken lightly.

The log of sailing vessels run aground on the shoals has not been closed. Each year new sailors learn the dangers of the light and dark blue contours on the nautical charts, running aground on remnants of ancient islands whose surfaces have crumbled and eroded away in events and storms not recorded by man.

Chambers Island has Hanover Shoal sweeping out from its southeast spit. It is a devilish trap, one and one-half feet deep and extending two and one-third miles from the shore. Pirate, Jack, Little Strawberry, and Adventure islands, as well as miscellaneous rubble just at the water's surface, are part of a peninsula that sweeps out along the north side of Fish Creek Harbor and hooks toward another old island now known as Horse Reefs.

Whaleback Shoal is within three feet of the surface and halfway between Death's Door and the Michigan shoreline.

These rocks have been raised and lowered by geologic forces, shaped and sculpted by ice and wave, and now give birth to white foam breakers as they trip wind-driven currents.

Sailing around these islands is a special blend of sun, wave, and wind. There is a link between captain and planet when the sheets feel the tug of the wind and the tiller shivers from the pressure of the water. It is an experience wrapped in a special language, and each term is a picture of action and motion. Tacking, listing, reefing, luffing, beating, and broaching — each word expresses an image.

A sun-warmed deck, with white sails full and symmetrical, a wave washed bow, the yaw and the pitch, are all part of a freedom. To catch a wind and see the horizon roll past, or to maneuver through the wind shadows and wind channels of the islands is to be part of Green Bay.

Sailing is a timeless feeling, a union with the kindred spirits of Norse, Egyptian, and forgotten sailing peoples throughout history. The equipment changes and the landscape is altered, but the essence is the same.

Green Bay is part of the magic of the landscape, and the landscape is part of the magic of Green Bay. This is the marriage of land and water. Each enhances the other, and the sailboat becomes a part of the natural forces of the day.

FRUITS OF THE LAND

THERE IS SOMETHING SPECIAL ABOUT THE ORCHARDS THAT BEGINS WITH THE REDDISH STEMS AND SWELLING BUDS OF SPRING. THERE IS A RED GLOW TO THE LEAFLESS ROWS, AN AURA OF EXPECTANCY THAT LIGHTS UP A GREY DAMP DAY WHEN THE SKY SEEMS THICK AND THE NEW SPRING GREENS LOOK RICH AND FULL.

OTHER FIELDS CANNOT GIVE THIS FEELING; ONLY ORCHARDS WITH A BACKDROP OF FORESTS CAN. AND ON THE DAY THE BLOSSOMS BURST, you wish you were a bluebird or indigo bunting to sit atop the branches and proclaim in song the moment of new life. The woods have signaled their newness in trillium and hepatica, and the wood thrush can flute in the glens; but for the fields the cherry blossoms are the banners of fertility.

Is this what attracts people to Door County, what makes this thumb of land such a popular summer retreat? Or is it the seascape, the fantasy of island life, the rich green woods, the feeling of an art colony, the fish boils, or the diversity of architecture that mirrors the past?

It may be easier to see why people return than to guess why people go there initially. My own first visit was a childhood ride with parents and grandparents to get cherries. Little lingers in thoughts from that trip except the swiping of cherries on the way home. The longer the ride the more you must buy, for no healthy boy can resist the sweet-tart flavor of cherries when they share the same car.

There is a certain brightness, a joy that comes from that first squirt of cherry juice when the teeth pierce its skin. Who can be sad chewing the moist cherry meat or sucking the last droplets of flavor from the pit?

The pit is the reason the trees become laden with green balls that soak up solar energy and the moisture of the ground; they are sky fruits that deepen in color until they become beacons of red, decorations of midsummer. The sky and branches have more birds as fledglings join parents, and only the glowing goldfinch is left to sing his "potato chip" song and set up a nest.

This is the time for cherry-stained lips, clown smiles of red painted on cheeks by cherry juice. The land is sweet with cherries and honey, and the land must mellow as the fruits disappear.

The cherry orchards and crab apple trees lose their fruit in summer, but most apple trees reserve their vigor and add their color to a fall forest rainbow. Stored in the fruit are labors of honeybees; spring rains, summer heat, and cooling cloudbursts are held within its skin.

When the frost settles in and the leaves crackle and the puddles shatter under a morning step, the time is right. The air is clear, cool, and invigorating. Sounds carry well, and the crisp crunch of a juicy apple echoes like a symphony to fall; the senses of smell, taste, and hearing are all exercised in the apple's demise.

Unfortunately, orchards have been left to go fallow in some places, and Door County is now less an orchard than it was when I first visited the land. When orchards are replaced by development or standard farming, the region loses a lot. The best news I have had is that some people are currently using organic farming methods to reclaim some orchards.

My second memory of Door County is a visit with my young and beautiful bride. We were broke, like many couples, searching for a retreat with the proper perspective for love; and we journeyed to this area for a short escape, much like the visitors I see today.

It was a pleasant time in many ways, but it also gave me a picture of human influence that was upsetting. It was the year of the alewives, small fish that journeyed up the St. Lawrence Seaway like the lamprey and raised havoc with the Great Lakes ecology. They died in the millions that year and lined the beaches with their fetid rotting bodies.

They were the consequence of shortsightedness, lack of ecological awareness. They detracted from the coastline, the rich and diversified landscape that dominates local art and visitor's images. Even the gulls lost their air of gaiety in the gluttony that surrounded them. Anything can be overdone. The gulls sensed that. Any further insult to the shorelines of Door, like more development or deterioration of the water, would be too much.

DOOR IS A SEASCAPE, AN OCEAN VISTA WITHOUT THE TASTE OF SALT. GULLS BACKLIT BY THE SUN OR FOLLOWING FISHING VESSELS IN ROILING, RAUCOUS FLOCKS — PUFFY WHITE SAILS OR GAY SPINNAKERS ON THE HORIZON ARE ALL PART OF THE EXPERIENCE AND THE IMAGE OF THIS LAND.

THE Shoreline

A wave-swept beach at Sevastopol is a mental Caribbean, and the sprawl of the Whitefish Dunes behind the beach is an exotic sand castle. Waves roll in from Chicago and spill on the shore with new sands dredged from the bottom.

Here the beach moves back and forth with a geologic restlessness. Minerals that were once locked in volcanic rocks have traveled through time in constant change. What could be more stable than a rock?

The journey could have been from granite to sand dune to river sediment to sandstone and back to dunes, and the tale is far from over. Lie on your belly and watch the dunes' movement.

Dunes do not march, they leapfrog. Slowly, imperceptibly, the front moves to the back, over and over again, until a scattered seed sprouts and ties the grains together with a root; and that seedling becomes an anchor to which other plants can cling. And they, in turn, become an island of vegetation, a beginning of a carpet of plants that can cover and hold the restless land.

There are pioneer plants here, plants that

brave the sands and start the first small footholds. They are scattered by the wind and will often be blown too far or covered by a surge of sand. The battle is continuous and unpredictable.

Poison ivy is a good pioneer on dunes. Maybe that is fitting, for this tenacious plant also discourages people — the great eroders. With the poison ivy are patches of starry false Solomon's-seal which has a spike of white flowers on top of an erect ladder of alternating leaves and, like the poison ivy, has green berries when it is in seed.

In another spot you might find a low-growing shrub spread across the sand like a plant octopus. This spreading juniper protects itself by deflecting the winds that would blow away its foothold, and slowly sends out the runners to colonize the surrounding area. These runners act like snowfences for the sand; should they get covered, the ends will act like new junipers and start a new colony.

Thin trunks of birch, aspen, and hazel indicate that the sand dune is being slowed down. Ceaseless motion is changing dunes into a forest. With little effort you can find a nearby hillside of balsam, hemlock, and yellow birch. Beneath is a dune long ago locked into silence.

This seascape is not all dunes and shifting sands. In places nearby the rocks stand defiantly against the ceaseless roll of the lake waters; and spouts of water, slapping waves, and inundating sprays are the result of wind, rock, and water.

Cave Point is such a spot.

Cave Point brings mental images of a peninsula that houses a dark meandering cavity, but the caves here are different. No vampires, no ghouls of the night inhabit this area, just the ghosts and spirits of seamen caught in storms and dashed upon the shoals.

On one side of the sea cave the rocks rise abruptly from the waters, often overhanging with smooth water-carved ledges. On the other the rocks are in steps that the water surges up and then descends in frothy flows. Between the two walls is the sea cave, a topless hollow in the rock that has been sculptured by waves and swirls of water for thousands of years. The cave itself is nearly round, surrounded by walls for all but a fourth of its perimeter, and on a calm day it contains bluegreen water that makes it look like a wishing well.

It is not the calm days, the bright sunshiny afternoons that make Cave Point, however. This land should be saved for the sullen, grey, foggy days or the blustery, stormy days. On my next journey to Door County, Jane and I visited the Point on a thick, foggy day — one that gives thoughts of London or Maine and foghorns in the gloom. We were there alone. Billows of damp air rolled in instead of big waves; and the water surged, gurgled, and disappeared at the rock's edge. The fog hid the rest of the world, and the rocks were wet and seemed to glisten in an otherwise muted scene.

My thoughts of that day were mixed. The fog made us seem alone in the world, and the surrealistic setting made my wife's image stand out from the grey background. There was a haunting spell in the air. The fog was not just Lake Michigan water suspended in the sky. There were spirits floating there. Seamen of the fresh water that had tested their mettle in the Great Lakes' storms and had lost. They were there. I could feel them.

Every Door County coastline, every port has an aura of antiquity. We each journey beyond the limits of our body in spirits that hitchhike on fishing trollers or full-sailed yachts. Where we give our vision room to wander, we do great things and go beyond the curve of the horizon.

Big red cabooses on black steam locomotives used to carry me away when I was younger, but now it is the sleek sailboat pitched by the waves, tilted by the wind, and accompanied by the gulls. In the fog you can still picture the full sheets of wooden-hulled ships searching for shelter along that coastline.

Cave Point, Moonlight Bay, Gravel Island,

Death's Door — those were names that meant something to the sailors. Could they avoid the shoals and find the range lights of Baileys Harbor, or would another wife tread solemnly on a rooftop widow's walk looking for a ship that would never return?

Lighthouses were necessary to Door County. In Baileys Harbor the range lights were a unique double light system which used both a light tower and a light in the upper story of the keeper's house. The two lights were an early tracking system for ships. If both were in a line, you could sail in safely, but should they be beside each other, watch out.

Other lighthouses are preserved in Rock Island and Peninsula State Parks, at Sherwood Cana Island and Washington Island. Working Coast Guard lighthouses are on Plum Island and at the entrance to the Sturgeon Bay Ship Canal. Door County may have more lighthouses per mile of coast than any other U.S. county.

Cana Island Lighthouse is located on a small island at the end of one of Door County's many dead-end roads. A limestone causeway, awash with October waves, led me, barefoot and with pants rolled up, to the island.

This lighthouse is a classic, a National Historic Site maintained by the Door County Maritime Museum. Built in 1869, the Cana Island Lighthouse has gladdened the hearts of many storm-tossed sailors.

New electronics have replaced people and the heroics of the 1870s, when unusually heavy storms broke waves over the lightkeeper's house and seven ships over the shoals. Families no longer live here, but their spirits remain.

Big water bodies, like all of the Great Lakes, are weather makers. Land temperature and water temperature are seldom the same, so air movement from one to the other is continual. The presence of water means evaporation and clouds and winds. Clouds mean storms, storms that might not even travel inland.

Storms on water also mean waves, and it is not hard to picture their strength when you stand on the rocks at Cave Point and let yourself be showered by the spray. Lighthouse keepers and early coast guardsmen saw many turbulent weather systems throw water on the shores. There must have been many a strained moment as they watched with spyglasses the rocking and lurching ships aiming for safety. The lighthouse keeper could only keep the flames high, and hope. The lighthouse keeper on Pilot Island recorded two shipwrecks per week for 1872—1889, a good indication that hoping was not enough.

The coast guardsmen of the 1800's stood ready to row surfboats into the vicious sea. They were heroic, part of the culture of this land. These were men the sailors could count on.

The unexpected occurred often enough to establish the name Death's Door or Port des Morte for the passage between Gills Rock and Washington Island. The coastline is littered with sunken remains of over 200 ships. Whether ghost ships or treasures, they are symbols of the past and intriguing spots for diving. The **Nelson**, **Forrest**, and **Detroit** are sunken hulls. The wreck of the schooner **Berwyn** and the demise of the schooner **Ottawa** are part of the spirit of the shore.

The fog carries the cries of agony from the men fetched on an offshore rock, of the ship groaning and rocking, and of waves booming over the gunwales and water crashing through holes in the hull. Time has muted the panic that caused sailors to dive into icy waters and desert ships that remained perched above the reefs long after the storm subsided. Generations separate us from the muscle-bulging rescuers that rowed into the face of fury, but the shoreline and the fog still share the incipient spirit of the lake and its challenge.

Cana Island Lighthouse

Returning

Bjorklunden Chapel near Baileys Harbor

Interior of chapel

RETURNING

RETURNING

Sailing, Green Bay

Sailboat moored at Ephraim

Returning

Returning

Pioneer School House Museum, Thomas Goodletson Cabin, Ephraim

Moravian Church, Ephraim

RETURNING

Dwarf crested iris, Peninsula State Park   Stairway of Eagle Bluff Lighthouse   RETURNING

Parlor of Eagle Bluff Lighthouse   RETURNING

ANOTHER FOG CAUSED A JOURNEY TO DOOR COUNTY.
JANE AND I WERE TRAVELING AROUND LAKE SUPERIOR WITH
A FRIEND AND ENDED UP SPENDING A WEEK IN
DOOR COUNTY. OUR TRIP AROUND LAKE SUPERIOR WAS
ONE OF CLOUDBURSTS AND FOUR FEET OF VISIBILITY.
THIS IS GOOD FOR MOODY PERIODS AND SETTINGS,
BUT A QUICK CHECK OF A NATIONAL WEATHERMAP SOON
SHOWED ME THAT THE SYSTEM WAS NOT ABOUT TO LET UP.

THE ISLANDS

The map also showed that Lake Superior had latched onto the front and that Lake Michigan was resisting its advance, so Door County became our haven of sunshine and frolic.

This was July, and the festive season was full tilt. There were fish boils, art fairs, shops open until 10:00 P.M., and cars lined up in all the little towns. Our friend became ill, and we got rooms in a boarding house near Ellison Bay where he slept while Jane and I sought adventure.

In our previous exploration of the region we had been intrigued by the islands. Door County horizons are studded with islands wherever there is a vista.

There are rocky shoals, like Gravel Island, that serve as gull rookeries; and there are tree-lined islands, like Chambers, that support an airport and family life. There are island state parks, island Coast Guard Stations, residential islands, lighthouse islands — islands of every size and shape right up to the community and island of Washington with its daily ferry service.

Islands have long been a part of our cultural fantasy. Islands are places of excitement like **Treasure Island**, or challenges to the marooned like **Swiss Family Robinson, Robinson Crusoe**, **Lord of the Flies**, or

Gilligan's Island. Hula skirts, bronzed Tahitians, and warrior outriggers are our **National Geographic** images.

An island seems alone, stark, a contrast of waves and breezes, palms and pineapples. We are intrigued by life that thrives there without help from the mainland. Most of us wonder whether, in fact, we could exist in isolation. Secretly, most of us wish we could try. That is part of the magic of Door County.

Washington Island, a ferry ride from the north tip of the peninsula, is a community that is surprisingly free of tourist traps. It is crisscrossed with roads that are excellent bicycle routes. The roads are rural and wooded, giving a rich feeling of Americana.

The open fields in summer are palettes of yellows, whites, and reds with hawkweed, daisy, and sow thistle; and the sound of the fields is a bubbly effervescence of the bobolink and the rich melody of the meadowlark. In woodland stretches the forest is slippery elm, yellow birch, hemlock, and maple. The bright greens of the canopy blend into a blackness as your eyes try to penetrate its depth. A red squirrel may climb a tree and stop head-level to raise its tail, stomp its forelegs nervously, raise its stark white throat to ease the flow of air that pours through it, and issue streams of invectives at any intruder.

There are other singers to enjoy, other melodies that echo in the woods. Near homes we hear the robin, the redbreasted thrush of thousands of lawns. The song is lengthy and always seems to fit our mood. In spring it sings a day-ode to life and stands silhouetted in the rising or setting sun. But let the sun not appear, let clouds cover the sky and rain wait in the woodland foyer, and the robin sings its rain song, its sad lament. Later in summer its frolicsome tone changes as a "chip" is heard. This call is businesslike. Perhaps it befits the seriousness of survival.

Near an orchard the robin's song is sung again, but this time it is more musical, more fluid. The notes roll into one another and seem almost sweet or syrupy. Like the robin, this virtuoso wears a black cloak, but its breast is brilliant red and its belly is white. This is the rose-breasted grosbeak. This singer is not a thrush but one of the large finches, a seed eater not a worm puller, and its favorite place to sing is in the treetops.

Near Jackson Harbor the treetops hold another robin imitator as well. A hoarse sorethroated robin vignette comes through the leaves of a maple. With a sudden burst of brilliance a bright red-bodied black-winged scarlet tanager steps from behind a leaf, like a performer leaving the curtains of his stage.

Biking around Washington Island can become a loop of various bird songs. It is the ideal way to travel here. Pedaling is leisurely, and so is island life. Why be in a hurry when you can only go in a circle? That axiom may be true everywhere, but on an island the circle is more apparent.

Washington Island roads offer more than one route, and the areas of discovery are more than enough to fill a couple days with adventure. I sat on water-smoothed limestone on the northeast corner of the island and looked across the strait to Rock Island State Park. Gulls and waves were little obstacles for my mind; this land mass was another extension of my island daydreaming.

The first time I visited Rock Island it had just become a state park. Jane and I rode a boat to the island with five other people. We were the only ones there. We walked the cobblestone shores, listened to our footsteps echo in the hollow buildings of the island's unsuccessful Icelandic colonization, and explored the woods and the flora that had managed to cross the watery barrier between it and the larger "mainland."

The island is small, braced with cliffs on the west and beaches on the east. It was the first land in Door County to be settled. People moved in from water rather than land and depended on fishing for sustenance and livelihood. Island life suited their needs.

But why Rock Island? With Washington Island larger and so close, why did they settle on this smaller shoal? Maybe it was for defense; it was easier to protect the island if you could reach all points quickly. Maybe it was because the lake was so close to all parts of the island. Washington Island soon became settled and wrested the population from Rock Island, except for the lighthouse keeper.

Rock Island lost its role as a community, but not its strange attraction for daydreamers. Sitting on the shore and staring at its limestone boathouse with hundreds of barn and cliff swallows gliding in and out of its skull-like openings, I thought of lines from Robert Frost's poem, "The Need of Being Versed in Country Things":

. . .

The barn opposed across the
  way,
That would have joined the house
  in flame
Had it been the will of the wind,
  was left
To bear forsaken the place's
  name.
. . .

The birds that came to it through
  the air
At broken windows flew out and in,

Their murmur more like the sigh
    we sigh
From too much dwelling on what
    has been.
    . . .

For them there was really nothing
    sad.
But though they rejoiced in the
    nest they kept,
One had to be versed in country
    things
Not to believe the phoebes wept.

Being a more pragmatic human species, I reason longer and with more passion, attempting to envision a Chicago millionaire who would buy an island and try to establish an Icelandic kingdom there. Maybe Rock Island was chosen because of its history and the legends of this area's Icelandic past, maybe because it was secluded yet close enough to land to be near supplies.

In some ways that aborted dream is symbolic of all our island images. To set up a kingdom within a nation, what better setting could you choose than an island where contact with society would happen only by accident or travel and not as a part of everyday social intercourse? An island is isolation without going too far. Perhaps Frost also put that best when he wrote in "Birches" of his whimsical desire to be apart from the world, but not too far apart:

I'd like to get away from earth
    awhile
And then come back to it and
    begin over.
May no fate willfully
    misunderstand me
And half grant what I wish and
    snatch me away
Not to return. Earth's the right
    place for love:
I don't know where it's likely
    to go better.

Was Rock Island a kingdom with a chosen population, protected by the nation that surrounds it? The best of all worlds? Maybe not. Like all dreams there was a flaw, and in reality it failed. Now that hollow boathouse stands as a statue to man's failure while the encroaching forest reflects the endurance of nature.

I have walked the woods and marveled at the sun-spotlighted Queen Anne's lace glowing in the dimness. I have stopped beside the path and sniffed the grand fragrance of the Canada violet which grows a foot tall along the path. I have looked up through the crosshatched pattern of hemlock needles at rich blue sky.

The woods seem oblivious to the intrusion of man. The forest that managed to colonize this hunk of rock has a history longer and more dramatic than the intrusions of people. This rock has been under an ocean, a glacier, and a lake; yet there is life. It is separated from the mainland, yet the forest continues here as though tied to the peninsula itself.

How did the trees cross the straits? How did Queen Anne's lace conquer the storms? What wind carried the first seed? What bird passed the cherry pit that burst into life on the rock? The island is grand, the history of its people is exciting, but life itself is the story of Rock Island.

From my perch on Washington Island I stirred with my island thoughts jumbled in my mind and walked along the wall of limestone. Overhead were cedars grasping at cracks and leaning towards the sun and waves. Embedded in the stone were nodules of flint — material for making Indian arrowheads, fire starters, scrapers, and knives.

The story of the islands must take a different turn, for the resources are not just fish and water. White cedar is one of the best building materials, a wood that resists rotting better than most, a deer food par excellence. Deer, building materials, hunting materials — this was an intriguing connection. Nothing in nature, not even man, moves without relating to something else.

Cedars grow near water because they cannot tolerate even low-heat fires, and water affords the best protection for them. Red squirrels, pruning the new growth and gathering food, knock seeds into the water; they float to other shores. The growth stabilizes shorelines, attracts browsing animals, and provides the ready conditions for ancient man.

Archaeological sites at Mero and Heins Creek show that woodland and Mississippian cultures were on the peninsula. They show tool making and a use of the clays of the southern peninsula. Were these people also island dwellers? There is no good answer to the story of the early Indian cultures. The cultures that were here may have been Hopewellian that traveled along the lake from Illinois or the Point Peninsula group from New York and Ontario, and they could have even hopscotched across the islands to the north.

All we have left to tell us of the early people of this land are a few scattered artifacts and cryptic messages from nature. Hemlock and deer and flint — what could they mean?

Beyond the Point there are a bog, a chest-deep cedar swamp, a hardwoods stand, and Jackson Harbor. The boat for Rock Island leaves from here, and so do fishing vessels. Nets dry in the sun, gull laughter echoes on the sun-bleached boards of old buildings, a few hulls of boats that are no longer serviceable pass their days in the sun, and a sunflower grows out of one of the old windows.

Hemingway would have found an energy in this port that goes beyond the docks and quietness of a village past its fishing prime. He would have seen poetry in the landscape and on the brows of old fishermen and the young who still seek a fading profession. The lake still rampages with the best of seas; and fish, though fewer now, still link a people with their ancient homes.

Whatever the hidden meanings might be, the pleasure of the port is certainly shared by many. Washington Island is a thousand such reflections of mankind and nature. It is a mirror that reflects while constantly changing.

Here once were French fur traders who had followed in the wake of Nicollet's birch bark canoe. The Winnebagos were here, and the Potawatomis came seeking peace. Irish and Germans were clearing forest land and building homes of piled limestone.

Farming and fishing were the occupations of islanders until tourism offered a third means of livelihood. Over the years the complex of people underwent many changes, and the land and weather tested their mettle.

In 1850, there were 169 Washington Islanders, and the heads of the families had the following nationalities: Irish — 9, English — 7, German — 5, Canadian — 4, Scottish — 3, Dutch — 1, Cuban — 1, and Santo Domingoan — 1.

From within the United States westward-moving pioneers also contributed to the census. There were 32 New York families, 13 families from other parts of New England, and eight from Ohio.

The most conspicuous absence was Icelandic. Legends of hardy fishermen from that frigid isle surround the island's history even today; there are those who insist that the Icelanders first settled Washington Island.

Even the 1973 Door County tourism guide tells how "Over a hundred years ago, Icelandic fishermen heard of fabulous catches of fish in Lake Michigan" and "others followed and Washington Island has the distinction of being the oldest Icelandic community in the United States."

The Island resources were not endless. Like the earth as a whole, these people had to learn to live within the limits of nature. In 1865, the food fish of the lake were declining. Glutted markets, use of fish for fertilizer, and waste had taken their toll. Times were becoming tougher for the fishermen.

In 1860, the population of Washington Island was 631. In 1870, it was 385. There was a town government which had been in existence for twenty years. Nothing eventful was to happen in 1870 except for the arrival of four young bachelors from Milwaukee who had just recently immigrated from Iceland. These early Icelanders were Mormons, not the popular Lutherans. They had little success with the land or the acceptance of their philosophy. By the end of the century twenty Icelandic men, some with their families, had migrated to Washington Island.

I pedaled on to Mountain Park, climbed the tower on this island highland and looked out in all directions to solidify my impressions of Washington Island. From here I could see the ferry line to Gills Rock, the protected bay of Jackson Harbor, Rock Island and its lighthouse, Boyers Bluff, the magnificent palisade at the west side of the island, the woodlands, and the farmlands.

In the northwest corner was Little Lake, a wooded lake as beautiful as any on the mainland and yet more inspiring than many because of its position as a lake within a lake. It is a unique setting that deserves protection from development. I met great blue herons there, and I was even rude enough to disturb a slumbering black-crowned night heron that belched its non-musical notes at me and unwound from the branches to flap across the waters and settle on the far shoreline. Frogs moved from near my feet, confident that I had been sent to rid them of the great frog eater and knowing that since that was my destiny, I deserved no thanks.

There were old churches, old homes, and old graves scattered along the island roads — reminders of our mortality. In the background of my mind was a historic picture of Washington Island. There were wooden buildings with some snow-clad roofs, limestone chimneys billowing smoke, boats floating in a mass of white and waiting for ice out. Pickets of wood stuck out in contrast to the ground, and rows of cut logs testified to a preparedness of the people. There was nobody in the picture, no evidence that more than spirits dwelt here.

I thought of the pioneering spirit, the bleakness of that cloudy winter day, and the test of this land. What was it like to live on an island? I remembered Ben Johnson, an eighty-year-old fisherman, and his wife of three-months whom I had met on the ferry. They talked of island life, the real island life when the tourists are gone and islanders are free to do as they want. They talked of parties and cards, of marriages and clubs. They talked as newlyweds should talk — everything had freshness and zeal.

But the Lake — that was in Ben's eyes and in his hands. He had fished from Washington Island to Manitou Island, 41 miles. He talked of the good days, with the satisfaction of someone who had challenged himself. Things were different now — he didn't say that, but you knew that he thought it. The fishing contest held every year was good, but it did not kindle his mind as talk of the profession did.

Things had changed, but not all things. The Lake was still unpredictable at times, unharnessable and downright obstinate; and when it hit, it wasn't the sound, the waves, the danger that got you, it was worse. "Seasickness, it's the worst thing there is. I'd rather get thrown overboard."

I tried to picture the island as it must have looked to the first settlers. That was impossible; my thoughts strayed to Colonel John Miller and the naming of the island.

He had three schooners that plied the Great Lakes after the War of 1812. They were the **Washington**, the **Wayne**, and the **Mink**. In 1816, they set off toward Green Bay to secure a fort and on the way landed at Washington Island, known then as Potawotomie Island. They were convinced that they had set foot where no other man had been; and, with the pomp of the presumptuous explorers of the past, they marched on land with flag in hand and declared the island "Colonel John Miller Island." Their name did not stick, but the name of the vessel that landed, the **Washington**, did.

No name, no image stands out more in my mind than the suggestive excerpts of

Washington Island history that hint at the popular views of King Strang of Beaver Island.

To the north and east in waters that became the State of Michigan's, there is Beaver Island, a Mormon kingdom that predates Chester Thordarson's dream of an Icelandic Monarchy on Rock Island. In 1850, just after the celebration of Wisconsin's second year of statehood, the islanders learned that on July 8 the Mormon Strang had been crowned King of Beaver Island.

The islanders were indignant; the net-thieving, fish-hogging varmint had gone too far. The Utah Mormons were in Iceland looking for converts. Where would Strang go?

Strang — could there be a better name for a villain? Beware the Reverend Strang — he'll marry all your women, he'll steal all your fish, curse his heart — that old King Strang!

Rumor had it that Strangites were involved in the murder of a non-Mormon fisherman; and the government had brought Strang and some followers to Detroit on charges of treason, counterfeiting, robbing U.S. mail, and trespassing on public lands. He was acquitted in court — but not in the public mind. Strang had published the statement that these islands in the entrance to Green Bay were "a fine place for settlement." This was in his own newspaper, and it could mean he was going to try to take Washington Island.

In 1852, **The Door County Advocate** noted the alarming fact that Beaver Island had as many immigrants as Washington Island that year. It also hinted at thievery among the fisheries as being the doings of the Strang desperadoes and that the militia should be called out to protect Green Bay. The worst news to the islanders came just before Christmas in the same newspaper. Under the caption "Distinguished Arrival" was printed the name and title "The Mormon Prophet, Strang." He had just been elected to the Michigan legislature.

The name Strang kept cycling through my mind, like the revolution of my bicycle pedals, as I tried to capture the energy and fear of the Washington Islanders. How could this island community be so obsessed with one man's presence? I stopped at the restaurant and bought a butter brickle ice-cream cone and then sat beneath an oak tree with Conan Bryant Eaton's classic historic booklets on my lap and tried to see the images in his writing come to life.

In 1853, Lobdill and Graham, two disheartened Mormons, left Beaver Island and moved to Washington Island. In a way this was a defection from the mysterious isles. Their hatred of Strang fueled the Washingtonians, and they declared that it was a good thing Strang was in Michigan waters since Wisconsin had recently abolished capital punishment. This way he could still get his just reward!

The worst horror story yet from Beaver Island came in 1854. Strang's own paper announced that polygamy was required by God's Law. Also boding ill was the prosperity of their fishing and their cordwood sales and the works of the Mormon missionaries. Would there be more people to join the Beaver Island 2,000?

Tension mounted. Rumors spread. One rumor said that a Mormon had attacked John Laframboise with a bowie knife. The northwest part of Washington Island was in arms.

"Mormon boats are off the harbor — they've got spies to kill Lobdill."

"How many have you seen?"

"They're waiting to come in and burn the houses."

Officer Westbrook was frantic. Justice of the Peace Shirtleff had left Little Lake in a rage and needed help. Westbrook pressed the informant.

"How many Mormons did you see?"

"One, sir." Laframboise broke down. The other informants saw nothing.

The rest of the islanders were sure disaster would still strike. Strang could hit any moment. "ACT NOW," was the cry.

Blizzards were the only things that could cool the island. The area's blacks had moved to safety in Canada, and the rest grumbled about Strang around the woodburning stoves.

In April, 1855, six gallons of whiskey disappeared from Westbrook's storehouse at West Harbor and showed up at Craw's.

"The Mormons done it. Want to cause trouble!"

A robbery hit North Bay. "Mormons," said Lobdill. He recognized Strang's boats. "I'll give $25 to every man that's willing to go to Beaver Island and whip the Mormons!"

Two thousand people are a lot of argument against $25. There were no takers.

That poor Justice of the Peace Westbrook could get no peace. "He was the soft one who couldn't go after them Mormons last year." Rumors persisted that his West Harbor property was being sold to Strang. Craw's men confiscated his hay. His property was threatened with fire.

Indignation arose again in 1856. Strang had written a history of the Mackinac Region — favorable to himself and the Mormons, of course. His surest sign of insanity was a weird idea that the straits could be spanned by a bridge. What a dummy!

"King Strang is dead!"

Lobdill raised a posse to join others at St. Helena.

"He's alive."

"He's dead!"

"Strang's injured."

No one knew the truth, but that did not matter. Fifty men stormed Beaver, took seven hostages, and fled. On July 3 they returned with 150 men and found that Strang had been moved by boat to Kenosha. He was recovering, according to rumor, but his disorganized followers could be run out. And they were.

Islanders were proud. Then the newspapers ran stories of suffering, looting, and terror. The Strangites were victims. The Washington Islanders were the criminals. Conscience was tweaked.

On July 17, Strang died.

I caught the ferry and crossed Death's Door, as many do every day. Looking back on Washington Island, I knew that the island's charm was in a time-brewed cast of characters, mixed with climate and geography. The end result was a spirit — an island spirit.

In the haze a fishing boat seemed suspended above the lake. Engulfed in clouds as it moved from the ferry, it became transfigured into the ancient **Le Griffon**, the ill-fated boat that LaSalle sent off from Niagara Falls in a time when the Huron and the Iroquois and the Menominee dominated the land. It reached Washington Island looking for trade; and after it left, it was never seen again. Divers still look for it; historians quibble over its demise and guess at Indian attacks and storms.

I prefer to think that it was the first spirit ship and that it has not disappeared. Instead it sails yet with the Reverend Strang and Lobdill and Westbrook, with coast guarders and lighthouse keepers, with Danes and Icelanders, Irish and Germans, Mormons and fishermen, and with the unknown sailors of the **Whirlwind** and **ClaraBelle**, and LaSalle himself with Nicollet, and the Chief of the Potawotomi guiding its course through the fog and stillness toward those who will pause and wait.

THE LAND AND THE WALL

THERE IS STRENGTH IN LAND AS CLIFFS ATTEST;
THERE IS LOVE IN LAND AS GROWTH WITNESSES;
BUT MORE THAN EITHER OF THESE QUALITIES
THERE IS THE ESSENCE OF EARTH AND LIFE ITSELF.
THE INDIAN KNEW OF THIS QUALITY WHEN HE SAID
HE COULD NOT OWN LAND, FOR INDEED HE
BELONGED TO IT.
DOOR COUNTY IS A COMBINATION OF MAN AND LAND
at its best and its worst. Many of the common tourist trappings that seem to spring up like a bad case of acne in resort areas are lacking here, but there still are those common blights that offer meaningless escapes. Escape from what? In another place these pastimes might be harmless diversions, but here the land itself is an escape from a pressured world. A miniature golf course or a drive-in movie is just another object to be ignored when seeking the spirit of the countryside. Door County is not an amusement park, nor should it ever be.

The heart of the country is in the cooperation of man and land, and the remnant monuments to this relationship. The log house, the shingled barn, the weathered wooden fence and the moss-covered rock wall are discourses on man and land that rival the words of Walt Whitman's "The Common Earth, the Soil":

> The soil, too — let others
>   pen-and-ink the sea, the air,
>   (as I sometimes try) —
> But now I feel to choose the
>   common soil for theme —
>   naught else.
> The brown soil here,
>   (just between winter-close and
>   opening spring and vegetation) —
>
> The rain-shower at night, and the
>   fresh smell next morning —
> The red worms wriggling out of
>   the ground — the dead leaves,
>   the incipient grass,
> And the latent life underneath —
>   the effort to start something —
>   already in shelter'd spots
> Some little flowers — the distant
>   emerald show of winter wheat
>   and the rye fields —
> The yet naked trees, with clear
>   interstices, giving prospects
>   hidden in summer —
> The tough fallow and the
>   plow-team, and the stout boy
>   whistling to his horses for
>   encouragement —
> And there the dark fat earth in
>   long slating stripes upturn'd.

The poetry of the land is earthy. The theme of Door County is rural. I sometimes think that Robert Frost wrote of Door County in his poetry. Of course, I also felt that Vermont reminded me of a Door County in the East.

I look at the miles of rock walls that cordon off blocks of land in segments of fertility, plowed land between, with woods held back on the outside and lichens and mosses and snakes and chipmunks growing between. These ancient lines are modern Stonehenges, aligned with the magnetic poles and carrying significant themes of sweat and toil, glacier and sea.

Who stacked the first limestone block? Is that row that disappears over the hill a cabin wall that got away — the foundation of a visionary who could not stop to make a corner?

How many beads of perspiration dripped from the brow of that dirt-soiled farmer? Were their fingers smashed between the rocks, was ancient blood spilled in this kinship? Conquer the land? Subdue the land? Live with the land! — that was the real way to survive.

> Something there is that doesn't
>   love a wall,
> That sends the frozen-ground-swell
>   under it,
> And spills the upper boulders
>   in the sun . . .

So wrote Frost of his famous "Mending Wall." The old rock walls remind me of those words. Is it a chipmunk moving through the rocks, a snake turning over in its den, or a deer that doesn't quite clear the wall that sends the top rocks to the bottom? Maybe it is frost or ice — the growing water, the liquid push.

Somehow the old rock wall with its vagrant field stones tumbled hither and yon is more impressive to me than the neatly stacked blocks of limestone that seem to stand in defiance of, rather than blending with the land.

It is the tumbledown, rolled-over rock that gathered moss, contrary to opinion and sayings. It rolled until a growing face was exposed to the proper light, and then moss and lichen were planted there by the wind. And where it stood atop the heap, another face stands decorated with red and yellow and green shields and blotches and carpets of moss.

The woodchuck lives here in his home beneath the wall, and he is the feudal landholder who surveys the fields before him. The fence is his castle wall. Plump, brown, and full of tasty herbs, the woodchuck is a field animal.

> My own strategic retreat
> Is where two rocks almost meet,
> And still more secure and snug
> A two-door burrow I dug.

Frost's "A Drumlin Woodchuck" was a creature of a rural landscape, a beaver-like gatherer of roots that felt secure and snug beside its den, for as it says,

> I have been so instinctively
>   thorough
> About my crevice and burrow.

Crevices and burrows are common in the rock pile, and chipmunks can hardly resist their tempting storehouses. But not all users of the rock walls are mammals. Meadowlarks like to sit upon the stones, put back their heads and sing a hearty song, with their black V-necks and golden chests glowing in the sun.

THE BUILDINGS

MY WANDERINGS TAKE ME TO MANY CORNERS OF THIS COUNTRYSIDE, AND I FEEL ENERGIES FROM TIMES PAST THAT LINGER STILL. NOTHING SPEAKS MORE IMPRESSIVELY THAN THE ARCHITECTURE OF THE SETTLER.

EVERY CORNER OF THIS COUNTRY IS DOTTED WITH ROUGH-HEWN LOG HOMES, SQUARE SCULPTURES OF PIONEER LIFE.

The logs are occasionally round, still reminiscent of the giant trees they once were. Now they are stacked as if by a creative wind, gathering moss, stained dark with earth and air, and filled with memories.

Inside you can find where the fireplace once stood. If the cabin was Swedish or French, the chimney would be inside the building; others put it outside. This was the central spot for cooking and for heating. It was the heart of the home. On a cool Saturday the fireplace might give off the scent of freshly baked bread in the afternoon and the steam of heating bath water in the evening. There was a warmth in the glow of the embers and a reassurance in the snapping of the pitch in the burning logs.

The fireplace was also a temperamental operation and a weather forecaster. A change in air pressure, wind, and humidity might alter the draft and send billows of smoke into the home.

The fireplace was the sun, the walls were the family solar system, and outside in the fields was the universe stretching to the horizon. The sun was warmth and light that witnessed sickness and joy, childbirth and death. It was the light for reading the Bible and other family books. The world was smaller in those days,

and simpler.

The ironworks that served as kitchen tools were products of commerce and trade, an indication of success and necessity. The rest of the cabin was homemade. The chairs might be solid chunks of tree trunk or cross cuts supported by legs of smooth wood from smaller branches. The bed was made of boards split from the pine and a lashing of rope. The cabin was the earth, with limestone rocks mortared with clay forming the fireplace, and whole trees and parts of trees making up the rest.

The initial design of the American cabin came from the Swedish immigrants to Delaware and soon was modified by each segment of frontier culture. In Door County many of the early cabins are square, a floor plan often called the English plan.

Since many of the immigrants to this area were New Yorkers, it made sense for the cabins to reflect their English heritage. The cabins of the Scotch-Irish tended to be more rectangular; and home designs were altered and changed to fit the mood of the inhabitants, their talents, and the lay of the land.

Their tools were limited, and often a log cabin

was built with only an ax and a froe. The ax seemed to be the all-American tool. It chopped the trees, trimmed the branches, hewed them into squares, notched the corners, and added trim. The froe split off floor boards and shingles. The hands did the rest.

As more people settled the land, more tools were available to be borrowed or were brought to community cabin buildings. The saw was used to trim the logs at the corners, to cut doorways and windows. If a pit saw was available, it was used to make boards.

The common method of splitting a log into lumber was with the use of a beetle and a wedge. Once the log was down, an ax would be used to begin a lengthwise split. Then a wooden wedge would be driven into the ax hole by the use of a hammer or beetle. The beetle had a large wooden head, often oak, and an ironwood handle and served as an early sledge. The pressure of the wedge would cause the log to split down the grains, and a wedge applied along this seam would soon separate a flat-sided board.

The beetle was also used to drive the froe into the grains of a log to split off shingles or clapboards. The froe was a long metal blade with a hole on the end. It resembled the end of a broad axe, cut off where the blade thickens. The flat, thick part of the metal would receive the pressure of the blow from the beetle. On one side the hole would allow for a handle that could guide the blade and twist it to increase the pressure of the wedging action.

An adz was used to plane the wooden surface of the floors and doorways. It too was a modification of an ax. A man could stand over a board, swing the adz between his legs, and remove the rough spots from the boards.

A draw knife, an auger, and a hammer completed the possible array of small tools; these were used for smoothing, drilling, and fastening.

The workhorse of the cabin builder was the broad axe. The pioneer could do the job with a plain ax; but, given the broad axe, his job was easier. This was the power ripsaw, the embodiment of labor-saving devices. The British form of the broad axe was like a regular ax with a broad cutting surface eight to fifteen inches in length; but the Germans, French, Swiss, and Swedish had their own designs.

The Germans, for example, had a goose-wing broad axe which resembled a giant meat cleaver, only the blade curved back under the handle like the open wing of a goose. The blade was flat on one side and tapered to a cutting edge on the other, with the handle slightly bent away from the flat part of the blade. The log would be laid on the ground, stripped of its bark, marked with a straight chalk line, and then pinned and scored with an ax in vertical cuts along its side by a man standing on the log. The broad axe would then be used to chop away the sections between scores. The flat side would be toward the center of the log to keep the finished edge square. The handle's bend would prevent the woodsman from cracking his knuckles on the log.

The first logs, put on a foundation of rocks, determined the squareness of the building. These logs were the sills and were the largest, strongest logs. The logs usually were smaller as they went up the sides of the building because they had to be lifted higher.

The corners were held together by notches or interlocking, overlapping logs. The form of notching varied among ethnic groups and became a mixture of forms by the time immigrants got to Wisconsin.

There are dovetail notches, square notches, saddle notches, and V notches; and all of those types can be found somewhere in Door County. Most fun, however, is the potpourri cabin, the community grab bag, where more than one type of notching can be found because many individuals worked on the same cabin, each with a different technique. In one location I even found hewn logs used for one wall and round logs for another.

The early builders were often lumberjacks, and their knowledge of the trees is still evident. Pines and oaks were long-lasting woods, but the pine grew straighter and taller and was easier to work, so it formed the basis of the log home — the log sides. Split shingles were common in early Door County and often covered the entire home. The roof at least was shingled, and cedar was the logical choice, even though oak and pine would have worked. Cedar split nicely and rotted very slowly, so replacement was minimized.

The woodpile also spoke of a reverence for and knowledge of wood. Pine burned too fast so it was usually used only as a fire starter. Resin-filled pine knots were stored for special times because the thick turpentine resin was so flammable. The knot's intricate weave was like a maze that allowed the tongues of flame to penetrate irregularly and the knots to explode in irregular bursts of fireworks that added festivity and pine scent to the darkened rooms.

The main woods for heat were oak and beech — hot, slow-burning, coal-forming woods that could provide hours of warmth. People who lived with the land could not afford to gather birch and aspen as fuel when oak and beech were available.

Now the log house story is scattered on back roads where the settlers lived off the land and in the towns of Ephraim, Sister Bay, Gills Rock, and Ellison Bay. The log houses were homes, churches, and schools.

The towns were also built of wood, in the woods, and formed a commercial link between the woods and the lake. The log cabin builders came to the towns to find supplies, to sell their goods, and to socialize. And they came for spiritual and mental betterment.

The schools were one-room buildings with lofts where teacher, travelers, and students could find refuge when the land became snowlocked.

FISH CREEK THE ISLANDS HAD BEEN SETTLED BEFORE THE MAINLAND OF DOOR COUNTY. THE TOWNS WERE NOT ELABORATE, BUT NEITHER WERE THE PEOPLE. INCREASE CLAFLIN WAS THE FIRST PERMANENT SETTLER IN THE DOOR, LIVING IN LITTLE STURGEON BAY FROM 1835 UNTIL MOVING TO FISH CREEK IN 1842. HIS HOME WAS A CABIN AS WERE THE HOMES OF MANY WHO FOLLOWED HIM. HIS SON-IN-LAW'S CABIN HAS BEEN MOVED FROM THE PRESENT PENINSULA STATE PARK TO THE RIDGES.

THE TOWNS

Founders Square has another old log cabin, that of Asa Thorp, who originally lived on Rock Island where he had been employed as a cooper. Black ash was the prize resource of the barrel maker. The bogs of this area provided that as well as a good port to ship from.

Asa was a visionary of sorts. He saw a chance to make a buck with a pier for steamboats to get cordwood. Fort Howard was a long way from the islands. Nothing served the ships in between until Asa built the Fish Creek pier. Fishing and farming became the main resources of this new port.

The town prospered. The Noble House, a current landmark, and other frame houses changed the look of the frontier. Woodsmen mingled with the fishermen, farmers, and shippers — and a new breed of people called tourists.

Paddle-wheeled steamers plied the waters of Green Bay with summer enthusiasts who were willing to part with $7.50 a week for room and board. The paddle-wheels disappeared, but the fish boil, another part of this social atmosphere, did not.

At first, boiling potatoes and whitefish and trout just seemed like a wise way to make an easy meal. It soon changed. The tourists looked on it as a local custom, and it remains a strong part of today's Door County.

Ephraim   While Asa was building his pier, another strong-willed individual was establishing a church at Ephraim. The Reverend Iverson, not intolerant of imperfections, led a group of Norwegians to the fjord-like setting of Ephraim. Cliffs and sea, woodlands and fishing, each contributed to their feelings of home. They were overwhelmed with the abundance, so they named their community Ephraim ("Doubly Fruitful").

I can imagine standing on Aaslag Anderson's cargo pier with a piece of hard candy from his store and the gulls floating on the bay or following a fishing boat. The Caspian terns would sit on the boards, majestic birds with bright red bills and a black sailor's cap. In the distance a large bird would hover, plunge, and rise again with a freshly caught fish — as one does now.

With set wings the bird begins to fly toward a large nest perched on top of a dead ash near the shore. From the cliffs another movement of wings catches my eyes. A black-bodied bird swoops on the strokes of a six-foot wing span. The white head narrows to the large yellow bill like a spear. The white tail fans and twists to direct the dive.

The osprey hesitates and begins to shift positions. The eagle is intent. The osprey reacts, releases the fish, contorts its body in the air, ready to use its powerful talons. The eagle, still intent, sweeps below the osprey, grabs the fish in the air, swirls and flies to its roost, while the osprey is still doing an awkward air dance.

These birds are still around, but not in the numbers they were for Aaslag. The gulls are still numerous, and life is still exciting in the bay. In my mind I turn from the waterfront. Cliff and barn swallows dart back and forth across my path. They adapted well to this invasion by man. Mud-daubed nests decorate the eaves and line the rafters. Flashes of purple, brown, and orange maneuver in insect-devouring forays. I brush away the gnats, wishing the swallows good feasting.

Back in the store I gaze at the variety of remedies, necessities, and conveniences. It is a clean store. No cigarettes or liquor on the shelves. I am reminded of the puritanical times when the mistress of the store confronted a sailor.

He stood gazing at the shelves, mystified by the varieties, yet positive he must be missing something.

Lizzie, Aaslag's daughter, approached and asked if she could help him.

"Where do you keep your playing cards and cigarettes?" he demanded.

"We do not keep either item in stock."

"Well, what do you keep?" he asked brusquely.

"We keep the Ten Commandments."

Such a conversation reflected a good part of the area's culture. We remember that a minister led the founding of this town. His name was Andrew W. Iverson, a native of Christianson, Norway; and he was also the founder of the Moravian Church in Door County.

The band of Moravians that had journeyed to Ephraim was part of a long sequence of religious persecutions and expansions that have been so common to the history of the United States. Their odyssey began with the reformer John Huss in the Czechoslovakian state of Moravia as a movement within the state church. It gained impetus when Huss was put to the stake and grew in international significance through further persecution of other believers.

Refuge was given to the religious band on the estate of Count Zinzendorf in Germany, where they gained the time necessary to meld their religious beliefs. From here missionary fervor divided them again to Greenland, South Africa, and Georgia.

The Georgian colony of pacifists was driven north by English-Spanish conflict and eventually settled in Bethlehem and Nazareth, Pennsylvania. More missionaries went abroad. Some Moravian converts were found in Norway. It was here that the Reverend Iverson was affected and began his own personal journey to the United States — to Milwaukee, to Fort Howard, and finally to Green Bay where, at the age of 30, he founded a community.

Soon after establishing himself in Ephraim, the Reverend Iverson agreed with the local parishioners that the minister should have the biggest and best house in town. The result was a frame house with a cattle barn below, a hayloft above, and a meeting room for the Moravian church services inside.

The Iverson house still stands in Ephraim, a landmark of culture and spirit. The Reverend Iverson was a master carpenter. The boat that brought his household possessions on the trip to Ephraim was his own creation, a 24-foot keeled boat called "The Dove" with a natural-sized dove carved in the bow.

Carpentry (cabinetry) was one of the skills that distinguished the Moravian communities. Solid, graceful buildings could be found in all of their settlements. In addition, music and the art of the silversmith were encouraged as well as education for both sexes.

Pastor Iverson donated land and a flat hewn, log building for the first Ephraim school. In 1869, the school was replaced with a white frame building that had a belfry. The teacher then had the pleasure of new surroundings in which to administer lessons to 64 students in eight grades.

I look at this museum now and wonder if any lumberjack or sailor had a more difficult job than this schoolmarm. She had to be a walking encyclopedia on all subjects with translations for each of eight grade levels, plus functioning as a counselor, disciplinarian, and community reference — all under the scrutiny of the local townspeople in whose trust she was placed.

The children were from families of orchard growers, fishermen, farmers, and lumbermen. Farming was imperiled by the thin soils and was not profitable, so instead the people turned to orchards.

A large cherry orchard once thrived where the Peninsula State Park golf course now stands. Grape vineyards were planted on Strawberry Island. And cherry and apple orchards were planted in Tennison Bay.

Ephraim had an economic history like Fish Creek. The most consistent sources of revenue proved to be the tourism, cordwood sales, and fishing.

The town's ethnic heritage is still important in this Wisconsin fjord. Each Midsummer Eve the Viking spirit dances to the Fyr Bal Fest, and the Viking royalties are more real in spirit than most would admit. Midsummer Eve is a time for pleasure. Perhaps Theseus' instructions in Shakespeare's summer festival still express the calling of the fest:

> Stir up the Athenian youth
>   to merriments;
> Awake the pert and nimble
>   spirit of mirth;
> Turn melancholy forth
>   to funerals —
> The pale companion is not
>   for your pomp.

Before leaving Ephraim, I must pause and listen to the slap of wind in the luffing sails and read the names of yachts that have anchored here and left their signature on the Anderson warehouse. Ephraim has set another tradition for Door County.

In 1906, Captain Hogenson's Evergreen Beach Hotel had attracted enough regular tourists to give impetus to the Ephraim Yacht Club and the first annual Ephraim regatta. Now the annual summer event fills the bay with colorful spinnakers and windsprit sailors.

"Hard alee!" Catch the wind, sail away, search for the spirit of the osprey and the eagle.

Sister Bay   Still farther north along the Green Bay coast is Sister Bay, a Swedish counterpart to Ephraim and Fish Creek. The story is still logs and piers; but, in addition, a grist mill, stores, and a hotel were added to the community.

The town faced a devastating setback in 1912 when a fire caused the citizens to start over. Maybe this is why I find less history in these buildings than I do in other parts of the Door. Fortunately, the fire did not destroy the culture and ethnic background. Today I can watch the goats being milked on the sod roof of Al Johnson's Swedish Restaurant or join in the Fall Festival.

Sister Bay was named by Increase Clafin for the two islands outside the bay. Because of their similarity Increase called them Sister Islands, and the two bays that comprise Sister Bay were Big Sister Bay and Little Sister Bay. Being the first settler in an area didn't necessarily make one clever with words.

His other venture in place naming was Egg Harbor where he found a duck's nest. History seldom sits still for such unromantic legend, however, and another Egg Harbor legend grew about two ships that entered into a sham battle in 1825. The bombs of the naval fiasco were eggs.

Sturgeon Bay   Ships and shipping influenced many places on the Door. Who would suspect that Sturgeon Bay would be the home of one of the largest shipyards in the world — that it would be the home of a sailboat company that handles over 50 per cent of the international trade in expensive sailboats?

Do Hans Johnson and Herman Gmack sound like yacht tycoons? What about Hans' son Palmer who launched the company's first sailboat in 1928 after nine years of building rowing skiffs and fishing tugs? The company has grown consistently since 1919 and is now world-renowned.

Three shipyards, a steamship company, a marine salvage company, and a coast guard cutter all headquarter in this location that was once known as the bone-yard of the Great Lakes.

Sturgeon Bay began as a fur trading post in 1855, and subsequently was a quarry for limestone riprap, a fishing village, a tourist town, and a center for orchard work. There were even ore and coal docks at one time.

The quarry closed, as so many bedrock works did, when steel girders became universal. Now when I walk the lonely platform of the quarry, it feels like an amphitheatre. Plants are trying to reestablish themselves on the flat, stone floor that is almost marbled from the use and refuse of quarrying mixes, with red cedar and birch in abstract designs that represent the love-hate, conquer-seduction of man and land. The walls stand strong and straight, engineered cross sections of an ancient sea bottom. Oaks glow in the sun, rivers of goldenrod flow along cracks, and silence is interrupted only by the crunch of a broken bit of glass. From the road this second layer is invisible. The strength of the bedrock, the thinness of the soil, and the energies of the past are not noticed.

Gone too are the fishing boats, the twenty-five or so that left daily for lampreyless waters. Now shipworks is an industry in repair, and the commerce is more like a ship-sized gas station.

The people are still in a lake industry, but the atmosphere is different from the time of the Turner house when Alexander Laurie, son of a pioneer boatmaker, built his limestone house in Sturgeon Bay. He was a sailor and a steamboat captain, and his home was built of carefully cut limestone, with dormer windows, etched glass panes, and space.

That house was a steamship on land to him, but not what his city wife wanted; and, therefore, the home was never completed. They left to move to a farm when he retired; but the water was still in him, and he returned as a tollgate operator on the bridge — a far cry from a steamboat deck.

The Laurie house was quarried of backyard limestone by Robert Laurie of Glasgow, the son of a tailor, an apprenticed jeweler, and a devoted shipbuilder. He and his brother were adventurers who traveled the world as ship carpenters. They built a boat in 1855 and went inland instead of out to sea. They left Buffalo and found Sturgeon Bay. The oaks and the pines were a paradise. Now, the Laurie home is an example of a craftsman's touch, a steamship feeling, and the rock of the earth.

Houses seem like unusual monuments to men of the sea, but they are not uncommon in the region. Sturgeon Bay's Harris house is another architectural study. It was the first brick residence in Door County, built in 1862 by the creator, lobbyist, and father of the Sturgeon Bay Canal which links the waters of Green Bay and Sturgeon Bay.

South of the Canal   Brick would not remain unique, however. When I wander the landscape south of the canal, I am confronted with farmland and towns with the Belgian names of Brussels and Namur, the Belgian or French Vignes, Rosiere, and Carnot, and the Polish Kolberg. There is also the large marsh called Au Grande Maret.

There is a different feeling to a land with names like that. Carlsville, Ephraim, Valmy, and Jacksonport do not blend with them. Indeed the country itself is changed south of the canal. The rural atmosphere does not blend with lake here. Instead, agriculture seems to be the dominant activity.

View from Potawatomi State Park

THE
SHORELINE

Sevastopol Beach below Whitefish Dunes

THE
ISLANDS

View from Peninsula State Park

Potawatomi Lighthouse, built in 1836 on Rock Island

Herring gull

Apple orchards, beautiful throughout the year, produce a flavorful bounty each fall

Cedar trees overhang limestone cliffs below The Clearing

Cave Point

Overlook at Peninsula State Park

Commercial fishing building near Ellison Bay   Sailboats moored at Fish Creek

Fish Creek from Peninsula State Park

THE SHORELINE

Commercial fishing building south of Cave Point

THE SHORELINE

Chester Thordarson's great hall and boathouse, Rock Island

Mark Weborg, commercial fisherman   Trout fishing near Ellison Bay

Weborg's landing at Gills Rock

Anderson Dock, Ephraim

THE
SHORELINE

Gulls over fishing boat

THE
TOWNS

Rock Island

Fishing from Cave Point

Fyr-Bal Festival, Ephraim

Midsummer fest at Al Johnson's Swedish Restaurant, Sister Bay

Dancing around Maypole   Rosemaling

Fish boils have become a Door County tradition

Logging with a team of Belgian horses

Many species of evergreens in the Ridges near Baileys Harbor

The architecture is brick. Belgian houses are solid square buildings made from the soil. Half-circle decorations, that are signatures of the builders, can be found over the entrances. Brick dominates the cities and forms the family house of the farms. I cannot travel these rural roads without wondering why. Is it just an ethnic design?

Cornerstones provide part of the answer. The dates are left on many buildings, and the years are often the same. Like Upper Door, this land was once wood and chinking too, but a change transpired here — a drastic, dramatic event that changed a landscape, an architecture, and probably the people.

One need only look across the bay to find the name — Peshtigo. The year was 1871, and conditions were dry. The winter before had been nearly snowless, and the spring and summer had been draughts. Clouds that did build up over the lake dispersed like cotton puffballs in the wind. The land was scarred by the harvest of timber, the forests were shambles of drying branches. Au Grande Maret was parched. The cattails, sedges, and bog plants browned without going to seed. The tamarack and cedar stood dry.

Farm crops would not grow. Livestock and wildlife were staggered. The pioneers of Door County could do nothing but wait for the damp air of the Gulf to move north and the cold air of the north to move south and collide over their land.

On October 8 clouds came, dark clouds that sprang from the forest floor and billowed like atomic explosions into the air. The clouds were not wet, not cooling — they were a thousand fires joined together in chaos.

"FIRE!"

Nothing could be done. The people could only watch the sky turn from copper to yellow to red to black. The air was motionless until the surging fire charged it with its heat, and a roar filled the void of the woodland silence.

Ash choked the air, noon turned black. The roar intensified, and the wind began to pound with hurricane force. Boards, hay, helpless insects, and trapped birds were hurtled in a confused maelstrom, while showers of burning embers marched ahead of the main blaze, igniting small fires which spread and further fed the large one.

Hell visited Door County — and Oconto, Marinette, Shawano, Brown, and Manitowoc. Over 1,100 people died, over 1,500 were seriously injured, and another 3,000 were left homeless and mentally scarred by the conflagration. 1,280,000 acres had been devastated.

People, livestock, and wildlife had been immolated. They burned in their homes, suffocated in wells and other places of refuge. The fires were from many sources, most of them caused by man.

What of the survivors? Who rebuilt Brussels? How does one begin again? The victims had to look to each other and to outsiders.

Telegraph signals were sent to Madison. The governor was not at home. In a small burg on the south end of Lake Michigan another fire had occurred — Chicago was burning, and it wouldn't be until Wednesday, four days later, that the people of Madison would know of the Door County fire.

Governor Fairchild was with the state officials in Chicago, and his wife took charge. She organized a group to get supplies and ship them north.

"SEND HELP QUICK," ran the wire.

Carriages of blankets, quilts, and clothing filled the railroad cars; the train was turned from south to north with relief for the Peshtigo sufferers. Federal rations and government issue blankets and clothing came north, and contributions came from as far away as Peru.

The people scrambled for their lives and organized themselves to start again. The forests of southern Door were gone; but the red clay remained, and an architecture of bricks grew up. Agriculture continued. A lime factory began to furnish crushed limestone for the rebuilding of Chicago, and an ice factory carved up blocks of Green Bay for export.

Today, the Belgian culture continues to be a part of the land. The Kermiss — a church mass, dancing and feasting — is still a harvest tradition; and booyah, tripe, and Belgian pie are part of the Fourth of July tradition.

Driving north again, my mind poured over the ethnic background of the countryside. There were schools and churches still, tourism and boats, and a sense of continuity. Names kept going through my mind. Asa Thorp, Increase Clafin, Andrew Iverson, Justice Baileys. Who was John Ellison that he should find a bay or

Joseph Zettel that he should have the first orchard? What dignity did Elias Gill possess that a rock and a town should both be named for him? Is the Cupola House, in all its Gothic splendor, a monument for Levi Thorp, that has now become overgrown with the wild vines of progress, telephone and electrical wires?

I stopped at an old cemetery near Fish Creek, again overgrown with wild plants that do not recognize the esteem in which we hold our dead. Lichens were growing on the gravestones, weathering them as stone is meant to do. The names and dates are still clear. No one uses the cemetery anymore.

THE FARMS

I MOVED ON TO MORE ELEGANT MONUMENTS AGAIN AND SOUGHT THE BARNS AND SILOS OF THE LAND. ALONG A NARROW ROAD I STOPPED THE CAR AND WALKED TO A LIMESTONE SILO THAT STOOD ALONE IN A FIELD. THE ROCK HAD BEEN PILED BY HAND AND CEMENTED WITH CARE IN THIS ROUND TOWER, AND I SENSED A MESSAGE IN ITS PRESENCE.

WESTERN FARMING WAS PRECARIOUS. BUILT ON TRIAL AND ERROR, LAND WAS OFTEN SACRIFICED BY POOR PRACTICES.

It grew and expanded as knowledge increased and husbandry became more precise. But working with the land was not enough. A farmer needed to understand the land itself.

New Yorkers, Yankee farmers, took advantage of the Erie Canal and the Great Lakes route to move west, and they fanned out along the Lake Michigan shores to clear the land, put up log houses, and plant wheat. Their practices were harmful, however, and they soon exhausted rich soil, just as they had done in the East. Many packed up and moved to the Dakotas.

Disease destroyed the wheat, and the farmers

had to adjust. Dairy cattle, which had almost been pets and the responsibility of the wives, now took on importance. Dairy farms swept through Wisconsin. The farmer who had to adjust from straight line farming to contour farming, had to adjust to milking cows too.

The dairy industry had more new problems, and the Wisconsin farmer had to adjust his thinking some more. Food was rotting, and the cattle had to be fed. Indians had used corn cellars for storage of their corn — cellars which were pits lined with stones and clay, covered with roofs of boughs or leaves.

The first farm silos were very similar to those

cellars of the Indians. The pit was lined with stone slabs and ashes or charcoal, then filled with corn and covered with beams and corn stalks. "Silo" originally meant a hole in the ground.

Then, a farmer in Illinois built a tower on his farm and filled it with hay. His tower was rectangular in shape, which is consistent with the farmer who plowed in straight lines, had straight borders and square buildings. These silos spread slowly, and square wooden silos can still be found in Door County.

By 1882 there were 91 silos in the United States, a number which did not represent a rampant fad. Many farmers had a problem with the acceptance of silos, that of fermentation. They were hard-working Christians, and feeding fermented corn to their cows did not seem right. As late as 1905, farmers in Wisconsin were finding some creameries unwilling to accept milk from cows that had been fed silage.

But silos did catch on, and by 1923 the number had grown to 100,000. Stone silos were the most common since many farmers had already depleted their woodlots so the towers grew with field stone walls 30 inches thick.

I drove on and stopped again as I do so often to walk and touch the beauty I see. A barn was bathed in sunlight, and air swirls toyed with the dust in the windows. The red that had glowed in the turn of the century countryside was muted, faded to almost a memory. Cedar shingles held on to the upper peaks under the eaves. Wood that had absorbed the weather of the twentieth century had shrunk and twisted in places, opening gaps between boards, and in other spots contorting to funnel in the wind.

There was personality here. The farmer and the wood had both left their mark. I am told that you can tell the nationality of the builder by the way the barn is constructed. The Germans built their log barns with round logs and spaces between which they filled with clay, straw, and lime. The Norwegians cut the logs square and used a minimum of chinking.

Both methods were used by the Finnish; round logs were used for the hay barn and square ones for livestock.

The log barns gave way to frame barns. There were English designs with a gable roof and a side door leading to the threshing floor, Norwegian designs with long steep roofs that almost touched the ground like an A-frame, tall Finnish barns with two stories — one for livestock, one for hayloft, and German barns which tended to be built into the ground and were called bank barns. The Germans also used a style called half-timber barns which meant the construction timbers were visible from the outside and the space between the timbers was filled with brick, mortar or stovewood. In southern Door County there are good examples of all these types of early barns. There is even a Belgian brick barn.

I stood outside an addition to a frame barn near Baileys Harbor and looked at the mix of styles. The main barn had a gable roof and upright planks on a wooden frame. The barn was old, but still functional. Time had changed the demand that the farmer put on the barn, and an addition was made very early in the farm's life.

A wood frame had established the size of the addition, and planks covered the peak, but the main wall was stovewood. Wood the size that is used to heat the buildings or fuel the stove was piled like cordwood between the support timbers. The wood was mortared in place, like wooden bricks, and often covered again with planks. Where the stovewood is exposed, a mosaic exists that looks like a field-stone wall from a distance.

Stovewood structures seem to be more prevalent in the German settlement areas between Sister Bay and Jacksonport, but are also found on Washington Island and at Gills Rock. The reason for their use is only speculation, but it certainly seems easier than splitting lumber or hewing logs. Their origin is also unknown, but the stovewood structures were common in parts of Quebec and Ontario. And in 1870, there was an influx of

Canadians into the Door County settlements.

On County Road N, I paused again to study the complex of log barns that represents a very complete farmstead. It reminded me of the axiom that the wife chooses the arrangement of the rooms in the farmhouse and the husband determines the placement of the buildings. Wind, drainage, contour, and house location were all important to the selection. Beyond the barn was the barnyard where lifestock could gambol, and within the buildings was the dooryard where people could play.

Beside a stream overlooking the bay, I could view scattered farms in the distance and enjoy the woodland that is left. It was a lazy day with airy cloud sculptures and clover scent in the breeze. The stream gurgled gently, and I had the urge to chew on a stalk of timothy. The landscape brought to mind the words of Wendell Berry, a poet-farmer, who wrote:

"I have never been able to work with any pleasure facing a wall, or in any other way fenced off from things. I need to be in the presence of the world."

Mark Twain said that a farm needed a creek for swimming, a hayloft for sleeping, outbuildings for exploring, and haystacks for relaxing.

My thoughts drifted to another time when these barns were new and the raising of one was a social event.

"I heard Eb's going to have a raising this Saturday."

"Yup, most of the town is going to be there. I heard people from as far away as Forestville might show up. It will be good to see them again. Maybe Sarah will bring that good chicken booyah. I haven't had any since Arnold's barn went up."

The skilled builders were busy laying the foundation of the barn. It had already been decided that it would be a frame building with a gambrel roof and cupolas.

The professional framer used broad axe and dog, maul and mortise axe, mallet and mortise chisel, auger, framing hatchet, saw, beetle, level and square to do his skilled labor.

The barn began with the farmer and his wagon hauling a score of field stone wagonloads. These might be glacial field rocks or bedrock chunks. Each wagonload of stones was handlifted on and off, but the labor served two purposes. The fields were getting cleared for plowing, and a foundation was being laid.

A trench was dug one foot deep and two feet wide to establish the footings, or a cut was made into the bank and the rocks were laid against the earth. The walls were to be heavy and thick, three to four feet thick. The stone mason, or farmer if he was skilled, poured mortar into the trench and then dumped in the stones.

Boards were set in the corners as high as the wall was planned, and a string was run from corner to corner as a guide. No forms were used, just a plumb bob, level, and lots of hammers.

"How many hammers you got there?"

"Four. Need them all too. My heavyweight is sixteen pounds, then I've got a 12, 8, and 3 1/2 pounder. Cost me 44 cents for the small one so I can't afford to break them."

Each rock has a cleavage plane, a direction and shape in which it will break. The stone mason knew and used that fact, but he may not have been able to tell the farmer.

No form was used, just a practiced eye. Large rocks were put in the first layers, and smaller rocks and greater numbers made up the lifting levels. Wooden frames were constructed for doors and windows and the top of the frames always went to the top of the rock wall so the boards wouldn't have to support the weight of the rocks.

The carpenter took over from this point and probably had half a dozen assistants. Two girder posts were in the middle of the foundation, and two notches were placed in the rock wall. A beam was laid across the posts and set in each notch. Over this and around the entire foundation, sills were laid. The carpenter would then stand on the sills, like the old cabin hewer, and notch them for floor joists. The joists were mortised on the sills, and the flooring would be put on temporarily and finished after the raising.

Then the real skill came into the project — the bents were made. The bents were the brace sections that formed the walls and central support for the structure. Care was taken to measure and cut mortises to receive adjoining members. Holes were drilled where members were joined, and pegs were inserted to hold them together and pounded in with beetles.

"Welcome Asa, Levi, John. The chicken looks great, Inger."

"Kids, get away from the nails."

"Sarah, you look so nice. How are Sam and the kids?"

The mood was festive. There was a raising to be done. Wagons rolled in, the women holding baskets draped in linens and the men dressed for work. Pigtails were pulled, and an occasional wrestling match got out-of-hand. Sometimes twenty-five or up to one hundred people met, talked, and shared with one another. It would not do to be idle, but to gather together for work, that was something else. Church was formal, but a raising was a festive occasion.

"Grab the pikes, men."

Pikes? Long wood spears with pointed stakes on the end were called pikes. One team lifted the end of the bent that was to fit the mortise holes in the floor, and a second group stuck their pikes in the top braces of the bent and pushed. The ends matched the notches and dropped into the floor, and the bent stood erect. When all were in place and the connecting beams were erected and pinned, the aerial acrobats went to work on the ridge of the barn.

"While they're putting up the hayfork and rafter, let's get some boards on."

Each man had brought his own hammer, and work went fast, especially when someone told a tale at the same time.

"Food's on. Come and get it!"

"Children, wait until your fathers are done. They've worked hard."

"What color you going to paint your barn?"

"Red, of course, it's the only color I can afford."

"Mighty fine bread, Sally."

"Hello, Pastor, thanks for coming and blessing the farm."

"You gonna get some lightning rods? They have some beautiful ones with glass bulbs now. They say if lightning strikes, the bulb will bust, and you'll know how lucky you was to have the rod."

"No, I don't think so, but I am going to have a star on the loft window."

"All you Pennsylvania Deutsch seem to go in for them hex signs. Does it ward off diseases and sour milk?"

"Nope, it just looks nice."

The boards went up easily, and the barn was raised. The carpenters would finish the roofing, and the farmer would clean up.

"It's time to go home and do the chores. Come on, Jane, Matthew, and Julie. Good luck with your new barn. It looks mighty pretty!"

A LAND OF RIDGES

THERE IS A PLACE SOUTH OF SISTER BAY WHERE ONE CAN STAND ON THE SPINE OF THE PENINSULA AND LOOK TO THE WATERS OF BOTH LAKE MICHIGAN AND GREEN BAY. I STOOD WELL ABOVE BOTH WATER SURFACES, AND CURIOSITY INSISTED ON ASKING "WHY?" WHY IS THIS PENINSULA HERE? THE REST OF THE LAKE MICHIGAN SHORELINE IN WISCONSIN IS RATHER UNIFORM, SO WHY IS THIS THUMB HITCHHIKING ON THE GREAT LAKES?

Speculation like that deserves the proper perspective for contemplation, and I had to move to Peninsula State Park to walk beside the limestone wall called Eagle Bluff and nestle my back into a shallow sea cave. Then I could let my mind wander through the geologic scale, secure in the fact that my body was anchored in time and space.

There was once a time of great seas that covered the whole of the conterminous United States, with the exception of the northeastern tip of Minnesota. Where I now sat had been under the sea. The existing land was sandstone from earlier sea beaches and shale from muddy bays of a more recent ocean.

That was 440 million years ago. The climate was warm, the waters were salty and shallow, and corals built great undersea walls. The water was called the Niagara Sea. Chain corals and flat, round honeycomb coral colonies dominated the area and would eventually be covered with more sea deposition. Around the coral reef were green and red algae that grew with thick limey skeletons which added weight and size to the growing wall. Mossy animals, called bryozoans, attached themselves to the reefs. Long tubular animals, called sea lilies, were found along with clams, snails, and the insectlike trilobites. This period also saw nautiloids, that looked like octopuses squeezed into conical dunce caps, and sea scorpions that were six feet long and had huge pincers for first limbs.

The waters percolated through the sands, and the corals solidified as relics of the early sea. The result was a rock called dolomite which was once rich in life, but now is an inert mural of fossils and time.

Above my head, 180 feet up, near the top of the bluff, were coral designs in the bedrock. My mind staggers when I recall that it takes 6,000 years for one inch of limestone to develop and that dolomite is limestone in which the calcite has been replaced by magnesium. I am leaning against 12,960,000 years of growth and change.

On top of the hill, coming into Ellison Bay from the south, I look at the line of cliffs and the vertical drop that it takes to the water. Driving across the peninsula to Newport, I am struck by the contrast. Here I walk the wave-washed shores where small cliffs of limestone reach no higher than my head and cobblestones stretch in long sweeping arches from one outcropping to the next. I stand on a point looking at Spider Island and watch surges of water move across the pitted floor to lap at my feet.

Why are there no cliffs on this side?

The Niagara dolomite is a hard, heavy rock that does not wear out as easily as others. Many times a softer rock will collapse beneath it; and there will be a sag, resulting in a dish-like formation in which the edges rise and "las escarpas" form along the outside.

A "cuesta" is a ridge with a steep escarpment on one side and a long gentle slope on the other. On the peninsula the ridge is seven to 20 miles wide, and between Milwaukee and the Illinois line a continuation of the same ridge is 25-45 miles wide.

Cliffs line the north side of the peninsula, reappearing at High Cliff State Park by Lake Winnebago and showing up locally near Waukesha and Oconomowoc on the way to De Kalb, Illinois. In the other direction the cliffs are also evident, but the line gets broken.

Chips appear in our porcelain cuesta, and only the whole pieces stick out of the water. Minor nicks occur as valleys where the Sturgeon Bay Canal follows the route of the old Menominee River, and again at Ephraim and Ellison Bay.

Bigger chips separate Gills Rock from Washington Island, Washington Island from Rock Island, and right on through St. Martin, Poverty, and Summer Islands. Then the edge becomes whole again, forming the Fayette Peninsula and part of the Upper Peninsula of Michigan. From Michigan the chips resume in Ontario waters and separate North Channel and Georgian Bay from Lake Huron, eventually weaving through Ontario and bending to form the rock wall over which Niagara Falls plunges.

I walked beneath the cliffs at Death's Door Bluff and among its shed stone. To the northeast was Washington Island and the chips with Boyers Bluff and other cliffs to continue the geologic story. Across the bay was Gills Rock where probably no one was speculating on the ascent of the Door.

I explored the water and the rocks and rounded each extending corner. Thank God for corners, I rejoiced; I cannot resist them, nor can I refuse their invitation. Each one seems bound to hold a treasure or a view of the end of the earth or some other breath-taking colossus. To retreat with a corner not turned is to refuse to live. Contrast, challenge, and meaning — and all the elements of mystery and magic — seem imbedded in the concept of corners. They must be gone around like mountains must be climbed; for they hold a promise, and that is the essence of life.

I reached the utmost corner where Green Bay meets the straights. Before me was the reddish wall of Ellison Bay Bluff and its forest of green. Beyond the shelter of the bluff stood Chambers Island, way down by Peninsula State Park where all of my thoughts first took form. And I wondered why Chambers Island was away from the mainland. Why was there a pinnacle away from the cliff? But no one responded.

Instead I looked down at a wave-washed plant called chara that had been deposited at my feet. Some call this green algae-like plant stonewart. The plant is bright green with a whorl of branches at each node and a natural crust of calcium on it which makes it a natural candidate for rock building and fossil forming.

Scientists have speculated on the evolution of this plant.

"It began in isolated ponds," says one.

"No, in sheltered bays," says another.

Neither seems able to win, but both sides agree that chara was one of the plants that began the evolutionary trend from sea to land and that much of our limestone and dolomite might be made of its remains.

My mental images see this plant returning home to renew its efforts at rock building to unite with its roots, the ancestry in the rocks. Will it become a wall some day?

The road east of Sister Bay is called Hill Road. I drove it one sunny afternoon and laughed as I saw that it cut the "hill" in half. A hill on the back slope of the cuesta seems inconsistent, but it is there among a sprinkling of similar shapes throughout the area.

I am a slave to my curiosity, and my curiosity is captivated by the land around me. I had to stop to look at the hill. I found it to be a combination of rocks and sediments, with a definite direction to its slope — the direction of the peninsula.

This feature is called a drumlin, a word that comes from the Scotch-Gaelic "druim," meaning a back or ridge. So we have a Gaelic ridge on the back of a Spanish ridge, and that deserves an explanation, which must come from a story as intriguing and earth-shaping as the Niagaran Sea.

The episode revolves around a continental ice sheet that spanned Canada and sent little fingers of ice a few miles tall into the northern United States. The glacial lobes in this region were the Lake Michigan Lobe and the Green Bay Lobe.

Times had changed since the warmth and salt-water spray of the sea; the water that covered the land from the north was solid. Temperatures were too cold for life to exist in Door County then. Animals that could migrate south did so. Others just died. The icy bulldozers scraped away debris and rock and rearranged the contours.

In the region of the peninsula the leading edge split in two with one gelid mass following an old river valley toward Chicago and the other a river valley that followed the Fox and Rock Rivers to the southwest.

The results were dramatic. The Lake Michigan Lobe was large and eroded the lake basin more than 500 feet. The Green Bay Lobe was lighter and less powerful and deepened Green Bay by 100-150 feet. This made the bay a "hanging valley," perched upon a higher plane than the remainder of the lake, causing this bay to have a different personality. In today's winters the bay freezes while the lake does not.

The melting glacier allowed temporary lakes to form between the ice mass and the ridges of rock that it had left behind. The lakes' waters carried fine clay material that settled to the bottom over centuries. The moraines, rocky high lands, were a mix of boulders, rocks, and sand carried from Michigan and Canada. A surge in the ice would sometimes push the clay into steep banks, such as Red Banks by Green Bay and Clay Banks in southern Door County.

On top of the Door, high moraines and stretches of unsorted glacial rubbish covered the recently polished dolomite. In addition, drumlins formed with steep faces toward the advancing ice mass, tapering the sides in the direction that it moved.

Some people felt that the ice mass reached a frozen chunk of earth that would not move for the oncoming colossus, causing the ice to stub its foot on the hard spot and slide up over and down the far side. Others theorized that the glacier's unsteady movement, once it stopped its southern migration, was like a cupped hand on the soft earth that molded tear-dropped hills beneath it. The result was a change of shape for the land — uneven till, hills and ridges, drumlins by Sister Bay and Brussels, and an esker by Rosiere.

The esker is another ridge and another unique word that comes from the Irish-Gaelic "eiscir" or ridge. The esker is a sand and gravel deposit from a river that ran within or under a glacier. Rivers did exist in the frozen ice masses. Waters would form on the top of the big ice sheets and carve surface valleys that we can no longer see. In addition, the waters would sometimes drop beneath the surface, much like the lost rivers of the southern United States that flow within the caverns of limestone bedrock.

Rocks that the glacier had pried loose and digested during its journey were now loosened by the erosion of the ice and dropped into the river valley. Where the water reached the bedrock, the debris would fall to the ground and mound up. It was like a river valley in reverse. The longer the river lasted, the more the rocks would pile up, and the bottom would raise the river to erode some more.

If the flow slowed down, small grains would be deposited. If it sped up, the smaller materials would be carried to the end of the glacier or to an opening within. Layers of sorted gravel arranged themselves in snakelike ridges, or eskers.

Still one more series of ridges outlines the top of the Door. I sat on beach sand and contemplated the past. What new and intriguing tale could be spun from this latest discovery? Let's just say "Welcome to Lake Chicago, or Lake Algonquin, or Nipissing Great Lakes;" but whatever you do, don't go running for the surf, because Lake Michigan waters are still three miles away.

Following the glacier, there was lots of water for the land to deal with. The water would melt from the diminishing ice sheet, fill basins the ice had created, and dam up behind moraines until the river systems could carry the water away.

While ice still stood in the Upper Peninsula and the upper fifth of the present lake basin, water filled the rest of the trough to create frigid Lake Chicago. The land was cold. Rocks and till were barren. Icebergs thundered from the glacier and floated past Washington Island.

The melting continued, and the glacier loomed on the Canadian border. On the horizon to the north it stood out like the blue shadows of the mountains that seem always to be in reach, yet are miles away. The peninsula became three islands.

Water filled the gaps at Sturgeon, Ephraim, and Ellison Bays. The beach sand was placed there then, 30-40 feet above the present lake. Woody plants began to grow, and insects moved in to pollinate them. Birds also spread their wings and sat on the barren landscape.

Seeds floated on water or were carried by birds or the wind. Organic matter was coming steadily to the Door. I followed beach lines around the landscape and back to Peninsula State Park where I had started my tale of geologic turmoil.

The highest beach line here is 60 feet above Green Bay. The lake was called Algonquin. The waters from it filled the present Great Lakes beyond capacity to the highest level they had ever achieved. The Upper Peninsula was drowned, Hurons Island was under water, and the water extended north from Georgian Bay and Lake Superior to the foot of the glacial mass.

I walked down four more beach terraces, levels where Algonquin had stabilized temporarily in its melt and drainage, and like magic I was in the Nipissing Great Lakes. The peninsula was out of water except for its surrounding fringe, and the Upper Peninsula was back. The level was near the lake's present one, but the Sioux Narrows and Michilimackinac were flooded.

Three more beach lines, and I met Lake Michigan. It was the present. Beach ridges had been left, and in some places flat terraces of lake deposits were now dry and solid. Such terraces now hold the Horseshoe Farms.

The result of all of these actions is not just rolling landscape. There are sand, silt, clay, and rock, and combinations of all four. These primitive beginnings determined where the plants would grow; and they, in turn, influenced the wildlife.

When organic matter was added to the raw products of geology, it became soil. Between the grains are incalculable numbers of soil organisms, performing activities that change decaying plants to nitrogen and soil. How busy the life of soil is. Beneath our feet are millions of interactions, complexity beyond our dreams.

This intricate system still determines the ability of land to support life. The plants in turn affect the soil by the acid or base qualities of their leaves and stalks.

Diversity had been achieved. The mitten-like form of the glaciers and the lakes had been established. The weight of the glacier had helped the cuesta to form, and bedrock was available for homes and views. Clay banks were formed that would later make homes.

Ridges of gravel would be used for roads. Soils had their sedimentary beginnings.

Southern Door was shaped with the clay, and Chicago was rebuilt with the rock of Sturgeon Bay. The eskers were stripped to flat ground and used to fill the valleys with roads, but the people must be cautious with their zealousness. Door County may be "doubly fruitful," but it is also fragile. Too much use, too much rearrangement, and Door County won't be worth visiting.

The limitations of the land are less obvious, except for the impact of crowding and the barrier of too much development to a mind searching for horizons. The soil is the limit, and it has been since man first visited these shores. Early in Door's history farming was limited by the shallow soils. That has not changed. Limits of development mean preservation of the qualities we come to Door County to experience.

RHYTHMS OF THE LAND

THE GLACIERS DID NOT JUST APPEAR OVERNIGHT, NOR DID THE EARLY INDIAN JOG THE BERING STRAIT IN A SEASON. THE EARTH TURNED COOL FOR CENTURIES, THE SNOWS FELL AND STAYED, AND THE LANDSCAPE TOOK ON A DIFFERENT APPEARANCE. INDIANS LIVING IN ASIA WERE NOMADIC HUNTERS OF MASTODON, MAMMOTHS, CARIBOU, AND ELK. THEIR CAMPS WERE TEMPORARY SHELTERS THAT COULD BE ABANDONED AS THE GAME MOVED.

For them the seasons changed. The winters were colder and lasted longer. Plants were stunted by the short growing season, or they died. These people did not try to figure out the seasons. They just tried to live.

The Indians moved slowly seaward as the wildlife did. Musk ox and caribou munched lichen and tundra further south; mastodons and mammoths grazed in grasslands that had been under the seas; and elk roamed meadows between the mountains of the Big and Little Diomedes that had been islands in the ocean.

The hunter stalked the wild game in lands that had been under seas, just as we walk the Door Peninsula where a warm coral reef once grew. There was a glacier to the north that loomed on the horizon, and the Indian accepted its presence; for it had been there before his father's father and even in the stories of the ancients.

Many 35-year lifetimes can be consumed in a 100,000-year-old glacier. They moved from its path, but they did not know it. They moved like a deer will wander to a recent burn and nibble the fresh green shoots of aspen, not because they are on their way to something, but because it makes sense to do it.

The nomads followed the coast of Alaska, which was not icy, and down the Pacific Northwest. From there the paths diverted to the south and to the east. The glaciers had moved not only rocks south, but also animals, and along the borders were concentrations of offspring from native parents as well as transplants. For the hunter it was a good time.

The first Wisconsin Indians are called Paleo-Indians. They moved and hunted in small family groups with their domestic dogs and supplemented their diet with berries, nuts, roots, and seeds. Chipped rocks made points for spears with which to kill the huge mastodon, bison, and giant beavers.

Because of their nomadic lifestyle, evidence is hard to find to prove that they were here 13,000 years ago. The first concrete evidence exists for the Plano-Indians who roamed the land 5,000 to 10,000 years ago. A Carbon 14 dated site of an early copper culture was found in Wisconsin for the period 5,000-7,000 years ago, an early date for copper use anywhere in the world.

The Plano-Indians were not a new group imported to America, but a new stage in the development of the Indian culture. The name Plano comes from the shape of the hunting point that they used and the name of the locality where it was first found.

These people dwelt near glacial lakes, made dugouts, mortar and pestle, and used an adz. They probably found Lake Chicago to be an exciting homeland; certainly, there was little competition for the land.

Indian groups continued to advance as the ages moved on. Boreal Indians of the period 3,000-5,000 years ago were woodworkers and lived in the pine lands. They carved tools and polished and ground rocks such as they might have encountered on wave-worn beaches. They shaped copper spearpoints with sockets for handles. Knives, wedges, awls, axes, gouges, and colts were among the tools they made. Birch bark baskets, and possibly canoes, were modern additions to the warehouse. And domestic dogs were a part of the village life.

Lifestyle was changing slowly. Pendants, beads, and bracelets were indications of some leisure and developing self-esteem.

From approximately 1,000 B.C. to 500 A.D., these peoples were known as the Woodland Indians. Their lifestyles began to take on ritual and complexity. Burials and ceremonial activities dominated the intellect. The mound cultures, with elaborate burial effigies of snakes and birds, would develop in southern Wisconsin. The peninsular Woodland tribes that were to be the ancestors of the Ojibwa, Potawatomi, and Ottawa, and maybe the Fox and Saux, lived around Lake Michigan.

Indians floated the waters of Lake Algoma, another transitional stage in the complex evolution of Lake Michigan that occurred following Glacial Lake Nipissing, and a low-water, almost dry period before the present lake formation. These Indians rode the waves and cold waters in dugouts and canoes. They sought sheltered bays with easy landings. The Green Bay shore was not chosen because it was too rocky and dangerous. Instead, Heins Creek, Port Des Morts, and a peninsula between Rowleys and North Bay called the Mero Site, were three of the locations chosen.

Archaeologists have worked in the sands of these sites and have uncovered a story of the people. Heins Creek was occupied approximately 1250 years ago; the Mero Site, 1800 years ago. The pottery and stoneworks were similar to the Hopewell Indian culture of Illinois, the contemporary Point Peninsula group of Ontario-New York, and the Laurel group of northwestern Minnesota and western Ontario.

In the years 500-700 the Hopewellian culture developed in the region. They built villages and ceremonial centers, like Atzalan in Wisconsin, and located their villages along rivers like the Mississippi, Ohio, and Wisconsin, where they could have both transportation and food.

They were an agricultural people, but they also relied on hunting and fishing, and on trade. No early culture had so broad a network of commerce as the Hopewells. They traded for grizzly bear teeth and obsidian from the Rockies, conch shells from the Gulf, mica from the Appalachians, and copper and lead from the Great Lakes.

Ceremonial objects became important. They

made fine pottery. They wove cloth from the inner bark of trees to adorn their bodies. Sculptured stone pipes were made from kaolinite near Rice Lake, Wisconsin, and catlinite from Pipestone, Minnesota. There were even musical instruments to complete the cultural-pastoral setting.

The Point Peninsula group was a cultural counterpoint without agriculture. The early Woodland Indians of the region of the Door were being replaced by a Mississippi River culture.

Why they were so completely replaced is a mystery.

The people who lived on the Door were fishermen. On the Heins Site harpoons were found and a double-pointed bone tool that might have been a shuttle for net weaving.

At the Mero Site net sinkers and mat sewing needles were found. Bones from these sites revealed that there were crayfish, perch, bass, pickerel, northern pike, sturgeon, white sucker, walleyes, drum, and catfish as well as turtles, loons, grebes, swans, and pintails.

In the surrounding woods they could hunt deer, beaver, porcupine, otter, robin and other songbirds, marten, elk, lynx, moose, wolf, and bear.

Suddenly, the Hopewell civilization faded. In Wisconsin there was a fragmentation of culture groups. The mound builders of southern Wisconsin developed their rich effigy period around 1000 to 1600 A.D. The Algonquian language group split into the Potawatomi of lower Michigan, the Menominee of the Upper Peninsula, the Saux and Fox of northern Wisconsin, the Kickapoo of southern Wisconsin, and the Ojibwa of Lake Superior.

The Soiuan language group, descendants of the Oneota, resurfaced near Green Bay and are now called the Winnebagos. They lived surrounded by the Algonquian nation.

The name Algonquian means tree eater and referred to the inner bark cakes that these people subsisted on in periods of bad weather and poor hunting. The Ojibwa were the nomadic hunters; their name was translated to puffed seam, which referred to their style of moccasin. The Ottawas of Ontario were the wanderers who strayed long distances to hunt, trade, and make war. The Potawatomi, Saux, Fox, and Menominee were more sedentary and agricultural.

The Potawatomis were called po-da-waud-um-eeg (those who keep the fire), the Sauk were o-saug-eeg (those who live at the entry — possibly Green Bay), the Menominee were o-mun-o-min-eeg (wild rice people), and the Fox were o-dug-am-eeg (those who live on the opposite side — maybe of the bay?). Although each group was different, they had a common language.

To the Indians nature was always present. Throughout their history the different tribes had a remarkable sameness in their comprehension of the world. Some feared the world's ferocity, and others praised the earth's goodness. Some apologized to slain animals or made a promise to return the bounty of the hunt to the earth when they died, while others slandered and insulted the slain animal.

Persistent in the diversity, however, was an awareness of harmony that could be struck out of balance at any moment, even by the actions of man. The precarious harmony of the world was a dominant theme. Seattle tried in vain to explain this, when he said,

> Our dead never forget the
> beautiful world that gave them
> being. They still love its verdant
> valleys, its murmuring rivers, its
> magnificent mountains,
> sequestered vales and verdant
> lined lakes and bars, and ever
> yearn in tender, fond affection
> over the lonely hearted living, and
> often return from the Happy
> Hunting Ground to visit, guide,
> console and comfort them . . .

The Ojibwa found five basic individual and

social needs: leadership, protection, sustenance, learning, and physical well-being (medicine). They wove these into the fabric of nature. They saw a fatherly image in the sun which included the power of thunder, lightning, rains, wind, mountains, and fires, and the immensity of the sun, moon, and stars. They had a motherly respect for the earth. The sun illuminated, while the earth had beauty and nourishment.

They identified their clan with totems, signs of earth in the forms of animals. The totems related to the five needs of man and their cultural divisions; for example: leadership/chiefs — eagles, loons, hawks; defense/warriors — bear, wolf, lynx; sustenance/hunters — marten, beaver, moose; learning/teachers — catfish, pike, sturgeon; and medicine/healers — otter, frog, snake.

They identified with the land. When asked who they were, they could tell you that they were the wild rice people (o-mun-o-min-eeg). There was a rhythm to the land, and they were part of it.

But the rhythm changed. The white man came and placed a different set of values in the region. The first men to move into the woods were Couriers du Bois and Voyageurs. They were exploiters of the resources, and they intended to change the Indian from user to consumer.

The first to come was Nicollet in 1634. He was followed by Poux, Langlade, Gignons, Paul and Joseph Marin, Allouez, and Marquette. The balance of the woods was changing. The Indian sought more than he needed. The totems he had looked to as sustenance — the beaver, the muskrat, and the mink — were now taken for beads, steel axes, flint and steel, blankets, and rifles.

The change that came could not be controlled. In nature the balance that is lost is hard to re-establish. The Iroquois were pushing from the east and the Algonquian tribes shifted westward. The Potawatomis moved to Washington Island and met with Nicollet. By

1836, most of Michigan was lost to the Potawatomis. One of the "Three Fires" that had formed a loose confederacy to deal with the white traders was extinguished. Only the Ojibwa and Ottawas remained of the big three that had forced the Iroquois from Canada.

In the East the Dutch and the French were keeping the Indians pitted against each other in contests to control trade. Then, in 1649, the dominoes began to fall. The Senecas and Mohawks snuck into the area of Georgian Bay and shattered the Huron nation. Displaced and disoriented, the straggler Hurons that had managed to survive moved across the waters and settled briefly on Washington Island. The Huron nation would not be heard from again. They became refugees at Chequamegon and other forts.

The West was getting crowded with eastern tribes, and the effects were felt as far away as Dakota territory. Fox, Ottawa, and Saux had shifted with the Potawatomis. The French now put guns into the hands of the Ojibwas and called them Chippewas. They used the guns to defeat the Sioux and send them further west. They also fought the Fox and the Saux who spoke a difficult Algonquian dialect. During the French domination the Fox were forced from their Wisconsin and Fox River homeland to the Mississippi.

The Fox Wars of 1701-1706 and 1727-1738 had damaged the French prestige and forced the Voyageurs to look to the Ohio for alternate routes. The French had a lot to gain from the removal of the Fox.

In 1754, the Fall of Quebec meant the end of the French dominance in the land. Repercussions for the Indians of the Door region would follow. The British named William Johnson as the head of the Northern Indian Department. He had been a fur trader who had negotiated with the Indians of the six nations, particularly the Mohawks. He had helped keep the six nations from allying with the French in King George's War. His allegiance was to the Iroquois, which caused fear in the West. Even though he advocated a line beyond which white men could not go, the Indian tribes grew restless.

They expected the French to return. Instead General Jeffrey Amherst took command of the British and Colonial forces and issued orders that credit could no longer be issued to the hated Indian as it had been with the French. His agents were a cause of unrest.

In 1763, Pontiac led his Ottawa tribe and the Shawnees, Chippewas, Miamis, Weas, Senecas, Kickapoos, and Potawatomis in revolt. He spoke for the Great Spirit when he said:

> Why do you suffer the white men to dwell among you? My children, you have forgotten the customs and traditions of your forefathers. Why do you not clothe yourselves in skins, as they did, and use the bows and arrows, and the stone-pointed lances which they used? You have bought guns, knives, kettles, and blankets from the white men, until you can no longer do without them; and, what is worse, you have drunk the poison firewater, which turns you into fools. Fling all these things away; live as your wise forefathers lived before you.

British forts were attacked and defeated. The Potawatomi and Menominee struck the Green Bay post that was now under Paul and Joseph Marin. It fell.

Forts all over the West fell, and Pontiac led a siege on Detroit from May to October. Colonel Henry Bouquet saved Fort Pitt and Fort Ligonier; the spirit was broken. Detroit had not fallen as it was supposed to, and the tribes were defecting. Pontiac surrendered on April 20, 1769, with the following words:

> My Father, once more I request you will take pity on us, and tell your traders to give your children credit for a little powder and lead, as the support of our families depends upon it. We have told you where we live, that whenever you want us and let us know it, we will come to you directly.

The balance was still off-center and the dominoes continued to tumble. Another leader, Tecumseh, emerged. The frontier belonged to all Indian tribes, he preached. Land could not be bought or sold by individual tribes or people. Tecumseh said:

> The whites are already nearly a match for us all united, and too strong for any one tribe alone to resist; so that unless we support one another with our collective and united forces, unless every tribe unanimously combines to give check to the ambition and avarice of the whites, they will soon conquer us apart and disunited, and we will be driven away from our native country and scattered as autumnal leaves before the wind.

The Ojibwas, Winnebagos, and Potawatomis listened. In the War of 1812, they joined the British in hopes that victorious Britain would grant a permanent Indian state.

Tecumseh died at the Thames River in Ontario, commanding the right wing of General Practor's army. His ambition and vision went unfulfilled.

One more strong leader, Black Hawk, emerged from Tecumseh's troops. He had been angered by the treaties of the Fox and the Saux in 1804, which ceded all their lands east of the Mississippi. In Tecumseh he saw hope, but got defeat. From Chief Keokuk of the Saux he got conflict. The result was a war that never materialized, a skirmish that resulted in many dead Indians at Bad Axe River in Wisconsin in 1832. For Black Hawk it was prison and the indignation of being put into the custody of Keokuk. The time of the Indian had passed, and the rhythm of the land was not yet stable.

To this changing pattern of life a new surge

came forth — the pioneers. They moved to a peninsula where the artifacts of an Indian culture lay buried beneath the sands of Lake Michigan beaches, and the breeze carried the calls of the Indian to the trees like the hollow note blown across the mouth of an empty bottle.

I walked the paths of Newport State Park, past the outlines of the store and post office and the lilacs and grapevines of yesteryear's yards. In the woods are the remains of log cabins. Large logs still lay on cobblestone beaches washed by the spray and bleached by the sun.

The town of Newport was settled by Hans Johnson in the early 1870's. He was a logger and the owner of a dock, a sawmill, and a general store. There were about 25 men working with him. By 1886, there were 200 people in the town.

Steamers picked up lumber, cordwood, and Christmas trees for the southern cities of the lake. A stage came once every three weeks from Sturgeon Bay. By the winter of 1893-94, the population had grown to 300. There were now a flour mill, hotel, pump factory, shoemaker, fisherman, horse breeder, wagon maker, creamery, carpenter, and blacksmith, in addition to the property of Hans Johnson.

In 1895, timber began to run short. Hans sold out his sawmill and logging business to Peter Knudsen, who also took over the store and post office. But Peter was not so lucky as Hans had been. With the timber exhausted, the steamers not demanding wood anymore, and the thinness of the soil, people began to move. By 1895-96, the population had dropped to 250. By 1904, the post office closed, and only 40 people remained in Newport.

Knudsen tried again. Newport was platted, and streets were planned in a land speculation scheme that never materialized. Everything was sold to Ferdinand Hotz, a Chicago investor. The town became a lifeless place.

The wind blew through the vacant windows, slowly shredding the flapping curtains. Wood-boring beetles and fungus destroyed tables and chairs. Signs of man were fading, and the plants and animals reclaimed the land. Orchids and asters caught my eye as I walked, and in deep recesses of rock I could observe the lacy delicacy of moss and fern.

I stood and looked across Rowleys Bay, past the mergansers that swam in the water, to the wooded land that grows into a peninsula just before North Bay. I thought of the Mero Site that lies beneath the sands, and Seattle's words came to mind as I pondered the rhythms of the land:

> But why should I mourn at the untimely fate of my people? Tribe follows tribe, and nation follows nation, like the waves of the sea. It is the order of nature, and regret is useless. Your time of decay may be distant, but it will surely come, for even the White Man whose God walked and talked with him as friend with friend, cannot be exempt from the common destiny. We may be brothers after all. We will see.

AUTUMN BIRDS

THE KINGLETS FILL THE RIDGES' NORTHERN FOREST, FLITTING AND BOUNCING FROM STEM TO STEM WITH HIGH-PITCHED BUZZING AND CONSTANT MOTION. A DRAB RUBY-CROWNED KINGLET WILL EMIT AN OCCASIONAL **PISHING** CALL, BUT IT IS THE GOLDEN-CROWNED KINGLETS THAT SEEM TO BE EVERYWHERE. THEY POP OUT, BOW THEIR GOLDEN CROWNS, FLIT

to a low shrub where the golden glow of their wings catches the sunlight, and then they are off with their ruby-crowned cousins and the boisterous chickadee.

These are boreal birds, common to the Labrador tea and spruce bogs, who glean food from the branches of conifers. At The Ridges Sanctuary they are the autumnal guides on the back trails, adding life to the fruits and colors of fall.

The chickadee is a small bird too, but it seems to thrive on the harshest of seasons. As the winds blow cold and the leaves drop, the chickadee resounds with bold **dee dee dee** calls, and with its feathers erect, it seems to gain size and strength with the snows, finally booming its spring song on the snowy fields of February when most of the other birds are still in the south.

Brown creepers, nuthatches, and woodpeckers move along the furrowed bark ridges of slumbering trees, eating the insects that hide and hibernate. The creepers move up along the trunks, probing with curved bills, quietly foraging, while the nuthatches hang head down and race around the trees, like belligerent mountaineers, yodeling their nasal songs.

Juncoes are bold, black birds, feathered solar collectors in open fields and woods' edges. Their call is like that of the kinglet, and their identification is in the white outer tail feathers that flash in their wake.

There is a boldness in the autumn birds. The boldly colored jay, like the chickadee, is quiet in the summer. But stirred, perhaps, by autumn hues, it flies from tree to tree, shrieking its name,

Proud Mary shops and motel, Fish Creek

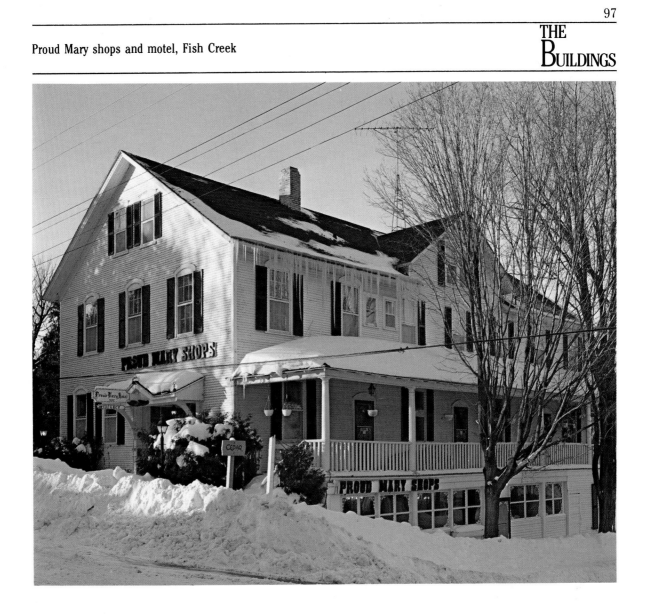

THE
BUILDINGS

Church in Baileys Harbor

Cupola House, Egg Harbor

THE
BUILDINGS

Morning sun highlights a country church

Schoolhouse Winery, Carlsville

Belgian-style home in southern Door County

Al Johnson's Swedish Restaurant, Sister Bay

A Door County dairy farm

Stone fence

Picnic area in Peninsula State Park

Asa Thorp home in Founder's Square, Fish Creek

An early church restored and moved, now overlooks Ellison Bay

THE FARMS

THE FARMS

Farm machinery becomes part of the scenery

Stovewood construction in barn

THE
FARMS

THE
FARMS

Farm machinery becomes part of the scenery

Asa Thorp home in Founder's Square, Fish Creek

An early church restored and moved, now overlooks Ellison Bay

Stone fence

Ferns in Newport State Park

THE
FARMS

Farm landscapes produce many moods

Hen mallard

White-tailed deer fawn

Red squirrel

Porcupine

Young long-eared owls

Horses near Gills Rock

Snowshoe hare

Red fox

Old fence   Looking across Death's Door from Washington Island

R HYTHMS
OF THE
LAND

Remains of cabin in Newport State Park

challenging all intruders, and proclaiming defiance to winter and mankind.

Many people dislike this aggressive bird. Is it because they are too human? They appear to brag, to challenge, to show off. Jays are role players, warning signals, whose blueness and boldness give pleasure to the fields and startle us in our complacency.

The birds of autumn are easy to think of in human terms. Their numbers are reduced, their variety is limited, and their behavior is overt. Many come to feeders; most dare to be near human hikers and homes. They suffer from being too familiar at times. Even occasional visitors can recognize the blue jay's call, though they could not begin to identify the delicate bell notes of its spring song.

I am bundled in wool, chilled by the breeze that stirs the sedges and phragmites of The Ridges' swale. Around me the golden plumes of tamarack sway among the cedars, and the surf calls to my left. The sky is grey, tinged with only a limited amount of blue.

I sat down to think, and a blue jay sprang into action. His bold lines of color, distinct wing beat, and loud cry brought life to the land and shook the melancholy.

Here on Door County Peninsula, a young minister's son sat on a pier in 1906 and listened to the call of a gull and heard the singing of the wilderness. Today the gulls, red-headed ducks, and oldsquaws of the bay still call and ride the gales of November. On land the autumn birds add their chorus, and like Sigurd Olson, who became the spokesman for the wilderness, we, too, can hear the singing wilderness in the flocks of feeding kinglets and their brethren.

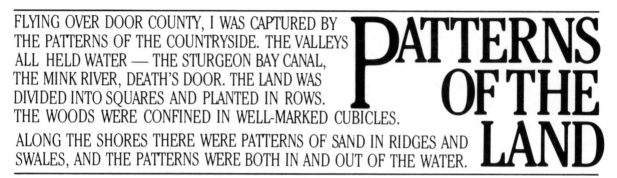

FLYING OVER DOOR COUNTY, I WAS CAPTURED BY THE PATTERNS OF THE COUNTRYSIDE. THE VALLEYS ALL HELD WATER — THE STURGEON BAY CANAL, THE MINK RIVER, DEATH'S DOOR. THE LAND WAS DIVIDED INTO SQUARES AND PLANTED IN ROWS. THE WOODS WERE CONFINED IN WELL-MARKED CUBICLES.
ALONG THE SHORES THERE WERE PATTERNS OF SAND IN RIDGES AND SWALES, AND THE PATTERNS WERE BOTH IN AND OUT OF THE WATER.

PATTERNS OF THE LAND

Continuity it might be called, but concrete evidence seemed better.

I walked The Ridges with my flight in mind, and I could picture swells and swales progressing to the horizon. Each bridge that crossed a botanical paradise changed the plant complex while also changing the centuries.

I saw a flitting flock of birds work up a tree from side to side, lower branches to upper and then down to the next. They seemed hurried in their movements, and I lipped a soft airy sound to call attention to my interest. A golden-crowned kinglet responded to my sound and alighted at eye level and arm's length with head tilted and legs crouched. There were white bars on its wings and a golden cap on its head. To me it was a kindred soul.

"Do you realize that the hemlock you are perched upon is on a beach line of Lake Michigan that now is an eighth of a mile from water?"

He cocked his head again, and I whistled softly to reassure him.

"Do you know that, unlike the beach lines of old Lake Algonquin and Nipissing Great Lakes, this beach was not left behind as the lake level lowered?"

He flew away without listening to my explanation.

Beside the wooden bridge I detected a banded pattern and stooped to say, "Mister water snake, perchance did you overhear my conversation? This swale you are swimming in resides between two beaches that once were covered by the waters of Lake Michigan. Do you want to know why it is so far from the lake now?"

He moved away with grace and indifference.

I walked to the observation platform that extends into the swale of the Winter Wren Trail and watched the whirligig beetles spin and twirl on the water's surface, waiting for the vibration of a helpless lunch. I knew they wouldn't care either. So I settled back and warmed my mind with the sun and played the drama inwardly.

The sanctuary that is called The Ridges is a special place for plants and animals. Along the shore willows and dogwood mix with rushes and horsetails to stabilize a strand of sand. Sand rush grows in straight rows from runners that push through the sand, and the complex of stalks acts like a snow fence to pile up beach. Silverweed also mats the sand with low compound leaves and bright yellow flowers.

Going back from shore, The Ridges have

balsam fir and spruce growing around mats of prostrate juniper and bearberry. The plants spread to hold the sands that hold their roots while small blue lake irises rise like sea waves all around.

Going back another step, balsam fir, birch, and ash mix with gold thread and marsh marigolds, cerulian warblers, and chickadees. The gold thread is special. The flower grows on a three-to-five-inch stalk that rises above evergreen leaves of three wedge-shaped leaflets. Showy white sepals surround a flower of slender petals and golden-tipped anthers, and beneath the ground roots of gold illuminate the soil.

Cedars mix with hemlock, spruce, and bellworts. Then white pine and balsam mix with Labrador tea and black spruce, and one of the very few boreal forest complexes in the region stands out on the ridge.

The Ridges, each one different, each one a beach of another year, formed not because the lake level lowered but because the ground rose. The earth that had been pushed and shoved by the glaciers had also compressed beneath its weight. The earth rebounded from its low point and gradually raised to meet the changing waters of the Great Lakes. As Lake Michigan stabilized, the land kept changing, striving for the proper balance.

Now beaches sit back from the very waters that created them and are a landform rather than a seascape.

The Ridges is a geologic, botanical, and ornithological preserve. It is not a people place unless you can be a serious student of nature. It is a living museum of nature and should not be overrun by the merely curious.

It is there because a lady named Emma Toft rallied the forces that could stall the development of this land. Then Roy Lukes became the naturalist who could communicate with the land, and an organization called "Friends of The Ridges" became the unseen force. The Ridges is one pattern on the landscape of the peninsula that will always belong. Its preservation is important.

In the land called Mud Lake Refuge I found more patterns existing, and I explored them with vigor. In the mud and alders I encountered a green flower, a northern orchid, and the subtleties of its beauty arrested me.

Another pattern swept my mind, and I thought of the contrasts of beauty and complexity. The green orchid was a sculpture of intricate design whose green stood out in the blackness of the mud and alder trunks with as much power as the pink and white showy orchids I had found earlier among the forest sedges or the yellow lady-slippers beside the red pine trunks. Beauty was in contrast as well as shape. Patterns are woven in combination, not with a single object.

I looked at the intricacies of the orchid. The lady-slippers seem exotic and enchanted, but their beauty is not wasted. The bee is attracted to the nectar inside the colorful slipper; as she parts the boot-shaped draperies, a rigid structure strokes her to remove pollen disks that she has carried from other plants. Then a disk is furnished by the host to take to the next lady-slipper. She exits at the rear of the flower and moves to another feast.

All the beauty seems designed for function, but Emerson's remark is still worth remembering:

> If eyes were made for seeing,
>   then beauty is its own excuse
>   for being.

The Clearing is an Emersonian extension of the Door County feeling for a few students each year who attend its special classes. It is the heritage of Jens Jensen, an architect, who wanted a school where adults could find the ways of nature in their everyday living. Mertha Fulkerson, a former secretary, was the one who made his vision a reality.

The Danish Jens was an immigrant in pre-Civil War New York with only a dime in his pocket. The rest of his money had been stolen. He moved to Florida to raise celery, found his way to Chicago and Kirk's Soap Factory, and wound up working in the Chicago Park System.

Fresh air and the outdoors infused him with energy, and he rose from foreman of Union Park to Superintendent of Humbolt Park and then, in 1894, to General Superintendent of the West Park System. He designed Columbus Park, built the first neighborhood playground and Garfield Park Conservatories. His innovative designs used stratified sedimentary rocks in gardens. His landscapes reflected both his personality and his sensitivity.

In 1908, he began a landscaping business that spanned the Midwest and Northeast. Then in 1924, he hired Mertha Fulkerson. At that time he was designing a school at Ellison Bay in Door County.

His philosophy continued to expand, and he firmly believed that man needed to know and preserve natural wilderness areas. He wanted a "piece of the wilderness" which would not be too large for people to comprehend, where they would lose their fear of the unstructured world and feel at peace with the environment.

In 1919, Mr. and Mrs. Jensen journeyed to Ellison Bay, followed a woodland road to a flower-filled meadow with an orchard and stone wall. From the meadow a footpath led to the bluffs and Green Bay. The Project of The Clearing took form, but had to wait.

It was dreamed of and discussed until 1934 when Mrs. Jensen died. Jens let his dream slip from him with her death; but in February, 1935, the 75-year-old Jens confronted Mertha with a decision.

"When the snow goes and the frost is out of the ground, I will be going north to build The Clearing. I have delayed too long. The need for such an example is becoming more acute, and one of these days I shall be an old man."

Following Jens' axiom that "In all endeavors we must start from where we stand, and from there grow," a school for landscape architecture evolved.

The work began, and Jens Jensen's prophecy came true. But he did become old and die. The dream would have died too had Mertha not rallied her energies and expanded the scope of the school to include all the humanities. With the support of the Farm Bureau a part of the Door was devoted to linking man and land.

Jens, like Emerson, wanted people to look at the land closer. Patience, perseverance, and preservation were all part of understanding Door County's puzzle. They are still the qualities that the land speaks of — if we listen.

Emerson said:

> Do you know how the naturalist learns all the secrets of the forest, of plants, of birds, of beasts, of reptiles, of fishes, of the rivers and the seas? When he goes into the woods, the birds fly before him and he finds none; when he goes to the riverbank, the fish and the reptiles swim away and leave him alone. His secret is patience; he sits down, and sits still; he is a statue; he is a log. These creatures have no value for their time, and he must put as low a rate on his. By dint of obstinate sitting still, reptiles, fish, bird and beast, which all wish to return to their haunts, begin to return. He sits still; if they approach, he remains passive as the stone he sits upon. They lose their fear. They have curiosity too about him. By and by the curiosity masters the fear, and they come swimming, creeping and flying towards him; and he is still immovable . . .

I followed the call of the ovenbird. He moved from perch to perch just before my eyes could glimpse his brown back and speckled chest. This woodland warbler is a partner to the flute-playing wood thrush; both like to use the echo chambers in the trees to amplify their songs. The wood thrush plays enchanted notes, suggestive of nymphs and fairies, while the ovenbird bellows eerie incantations with the strength of a feathered Pan.

The calls of "TeaCHER, TeaCHER, TeaCHER" bounce from tree trunk to tree trunk until all direction is lost and the source seems to be a clump of withered fern or the mushroom on a stump. Frost said the ovenbird is a "mid-summer and a mid-wood bird, who makes the solid tree trunks sound again."

Thoreau said that the ovenbird is a poet for "anyone can write verses during the love season, but the ovenbird sings all summer and the ringing notes are a pulse of the woods that says the wilds are alive."

These birds are part of a larger pattern. Speckled breasts and plain brown backs belong to the birds of the forest floor. Plain breasts, eye rings, and wing bars adorn the treetop vireos and kinglets. Birds of the field are splashes of color, like fruits and flowers. The warblers are darting feather-winged butterflies that devour insects that thought them swallowtails or viceroys.

Color patterns are encompassed in single birds and plants, but even more so they encompass the moods of the land. Spring is green and white, and there is a feeling of anticipation in the air. Buckets and bags hang on sugar maples. A cord of wood sits beside the stovewood shed. Snow moves back from the tree trunks as the dark shades of brown bark absorb the stronger spring sunshine and radiate the warmth.

Days in the 40's, nights in the 20's, and the sap surges to the treetops, and droplets fall from the spiles, filling the woods with sound as though telling the birds to return.

Yellow-bellied sapsuckers tap the trees in their own machine-gun fashion and lap the sap with their wick-like tongues. Red squirrels follow and revel in the feast. Sometimes they even become inebriated by the fermenting sap of the late sugarbush and fall from the heights of the trees.

Polypody ferns uncurl their evergreen leaves and come back to life as though Spring had a touch of magic. Color brightens in the conifers, and the snows part.

Downy-stemmed hepaticas open, as do bloodroot, Dutchman's breeches, and trillium until the carpet of the forest floor turns white again, suspended between two layers of green.

The green deepens, and summer is full. If we look carefully, we will see more shades of green than we might have imagined could exist. The lime green of the leatherwood shrub glows in the muted light of the forest, while the balsam seems eternally basked in shade.

The woods have patterns within that demand closer inspection. White cedar grows in a row, as though planted where only wind and wildlife could sow the seeds. One must look carefully to find the cause. Below the cover of earth traces of a trunk of a taller tree can be found. The parent had tipped and grown while lying parallel to the earth; but years added new layers of soil, and now the branches have roots and are called trees.

Cedar had been dubbed arborvitae by the Voyageur because the Indians used the fruits to fight off scurvy. Considering its tipover planting, "tree of life" might be more descriptive of its history. Perhaps the seed that spawned the original cedar was planted with the glacier, and the trees I now stand by are only branches of a nine-thousand-year-old plant that has succeeded in walking across the peninsula.

In another part of the forest I can find yellow birch standing on stilts like a mangrove removed from the water. Its seeds began on a rotting stump. The seedling nourished itself on the nutrients of the decaying hulk. Now, years later, the tree stands on root legs protecting the position where the nursery had been.

Other patterns unfold in the wetlands. Lake waves carry sediments that fill the entrances of bays; eventually, small lakes have ponds surrounding them, and large lakes have small lakes separated from them by dunes and sand bars. In this way geology continues — Clark, Kangaroo, and Europe Lakes are added to the land. There the green of summer reflects in the blue of the waters.

In middle summer there is a period when the sky touches the earth, and the fields are left with dabs of blue called flax and chicory. In the woods the moisture is sucked from the heavens in the form of blueberries and huckleberries. This blue is fleeting in most forms; yet the aster is a long-lasting star in the woods, and the gentians are bottles of summer sky in the fall.

Soon the dry part of summer passes and late summer yellows dominate the landscape. St. John's-wort and goldenrod cover the fields. August leaves begin to prepare for winter. The strength of the greenness is gone.

Goldfinches collect thistledown for the last nests of summer, and bobolinks are strangely silent. When the wheat fields are tan and rich, the upland sandpiper crowns the haystacks and fence posts with his figure. Summer vacations are passing, and chipmunks scurry to collect their summer profits before the winds blow cold from the north.

Then the season turns festive. The gala colors of red, orange, and yellow fill the autumn skies with a last celebration of life. The leaves of the maple are orange and rich among the yellow birch and beech, and the sumac looks like fire in the fields.

The trees turn first in the high lands where the frost can set in earliest, and the flow of colors eases to the lakes where the unfrozen waters act like radiators with their thermostats stuck just above freezing.

The reds fade first, and a gold and russet stage sets in. Earth colors, artists call them. Metallic phases of gold, bronze, and copper become brown. Birch bark, the red berries of winterberry holly, the bark of the willows, and the red osier dogwood are the last vestiges of color as the woods await winter.

The mood is anticipation again, but in a different way than spring. There is an anticipation of cold and snow, yet the inevitable seems slow in coming. Then the first white flakes fall, and new patterns begin to form.

TOWN AND COUNTY PARKS

THE STATE PARKS, TOWNS, AND RURAL LANDSCAPES DOMINATE OUR PICTURE OF DOOR COUNTY, BUT THERE IS ANOTHER SYSTEM OF LANDMARKS THAT DESERVES OUR APPRECIATION. THE TOWN AND COUNTY PARKS, FIFTEEN IN ALL, LACK ELABORATE STRUCTURES, EXPENSIVE AMENITIES, AND SIZE, YET THESE SMALL GEMS ARE A COLLECTION OF REFERENCE POINTS.

Some, like Ellison Bluff and Death's Door Bluff, have inspirational views, while others are only boat launches at the ends of dead-end roads.

Jane and I put together a string of small parks on a breezy, autumn day, and found each one to be a point of creative inspiration. These small parks are a legacy from a group of people with foresight, a group of people including H. R. Holand, Jens Jensen, Emma Toft, Albert Fuller, Mertha Fulkerson, Olivia Travia, Frank Oldenburg, and others who could see the need, as early as the 1930s, to protect the landscape of Door County.

Death's Door Pass Town Park is marked only with a green urban street sign that looks like a Chicago corner marker placed in the woods by pranksters. It is a small grove of cedar, birch, and maple, and a patch of algae- and lichen-covered limestone cliff between Gills Rock and Northport.

The park is a small spot only if you confine yourself to where you can walk. Lake Michigan lapped at the cobbled shoreline below us, and a blue jay sang and called from the trees. Plum and Detroit islands were reddish orange ribbons across the watery pass, and gulls performed the border patrol.

Here the cedars were the geologists, probing the layers of limestone with root fingers, feeling for fossils and fractures. On top of the bluff the hemlock and cedar seemed darker than usual because of the autumnal brightness of the maples. The woods glowed under thick grey skies from the sunshine that had been stored in the hardwood leaves over the summer.

The road to Europe Lake leads to a boat launch with a quiet dock, where one can sit and listen to the pounding surf of Lake Michigan on the distant shores of Europe Bay, while the same wind causes the lake to gently lap on the shore behind.

The road to Europe Bay Town Park was closed, but we hiked in past the construction work for a chance to look at the asters, knapweed, goldenrod, and

Queen Anne's lace that would not stop blooming until all hope of survival had ceased with the onslaught of deep frosts.

Creamy wolfberry and dogwood fruits, red rosehips, nightshade and bearberry, and blue juniper berries gave colorful highlights to a still-green ground vegetation. Flickers, chipping sparrows, kinglets, juncoes, and chickadees were active in fall harvest.

We walked down the road that descended through Newport State Park and ended at a picnic grounds on a sweep of sandy clay. It was a place for walking, sitting, and quiet contemplation, where the state park surrounds the town park. It was ours alone this day.

We walked the shoreline that now separates Europe Bay and Europe Lake, and moved south until the sand gave way to limestone slab. The energy of the large lake rolled up the sand, breaking over Gravel Island's shoals and down the point that separates Newport Bay. Hundreds of gulls, the real owners of Gravel Island, sat in the wind shadow of the willows and watched the waves roll and crash beyond the island's shelter.

A water pipit led us part of the way, walking along crescent-shaped limestone deposits and fluttering over sandy stretches. Tracks of raccoon, hare, cat, dog, and child told stories of past adventures, and driftwood, now landlocked, old pier timber with rusting stakes, and discarded aluminum cans all added more details to the land's history.

The Sand Bay picnic area is located between two sets of anchored fishing boats. The fishermen go out daily to gather in whitefish and chubs from the bays and waters of the big lake, returning with clouds of gulls overhead. The park looks north to the pristine shores of Newport and out to the open lake.

The boat launch on North Bay is a small area nestled between private holdings. It is a place to be quiet in, perhaps a place to launch a canoe and paddle the waterfowl beds and the emergent vegetation of the bay's north end.

The road in is a combination of farmland and forest, and passes through the quiet woods of Marshall's Point Nature and Conservation Area, where the sign states:

Please drive very slowly
Children, Hikers, Bikers,
Skiers, Ducks, Dogs,
Deer, Turtles, etc.
Have right of way.

Perhaps that sign should be a part of all of the roads through Door County.

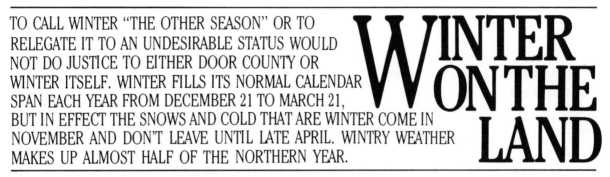

WINTER ON THE LAND

TO CALL WINTER "THE OTHER SEASON" OR TO RELEGATE IT TO AN UNDESIRABLE STATUS WOULD NOT DO JUSTICE TO EITHER DOOR COUNTY OR WINTER ITSELF. WINTER FILLS ITS NORMAL CALENDAR SPAN EACH YEAR FROM DECEMBER 21 TO MARCH 21, BUT IN EFFECT THE SNOWS AND COLD THAT ARE WINTER COME IN NOVEMBER AND DON'T LEAVE UNTIL LATE APRIL. WINTRY WEATHER MAKES UP ALMOST HALF OF THE NORTHERN YEAR.

This condition need not be bleak if you dress right and have the proper attitude. Don't think of shivering in the wind with icy toes and frostbitten ears. Instead, conjure up images of bright blues and stark whites, sturdy skeletons of leafless trees in natural art forms, and draping hemlock branches over a narrow ski trail. Think of blue shadows and red barns on a white landscape.

Winter is not a time to be avoided. It is a change of conditions, a new perspective, a means of seeing the land that was covered by curtains of leaves in the summer. Strap on your snowshoes, glide on your skis, wallow in hip-deep snow, laugh with rosy cheeks and mittened hands, and find solitude — the essence of winter, the salve for the soul.

I roamed this land in winter; and the magic I found, you can find. The crowds are gone. There are no three-hour lines waiting to get into Peninsula State Park, no traffic jams in Ephraim, no five-mile lines to take the ferry to Washington Island. There is more freedom to roam and less pressure to shop.

The Sevastopol Dunes were draped in snow. The image from the top of the dunes was one wide expanse of blue, a sheet of harbor ice, and a crescent of white beach. Swells of water had surged beneath the ice and raised great windrows until they could no longer support the weight and cracked beneath the stress.

The ice sheets moved back and forth, and the cracks enlarged to open ponds where mergansers, scoters, goldeneyes, and buffleheads consorted. The ice hit upon itself and chimed in the empty bay. The sheets shifted and closed, only to open again in another spot.

White-winged scoters swam along the ice-edge and dove for food beneath the glass, while larger mergansers swam and dove and occasionally raised up on their tails, stretched their wings, and flashed a coat of black and white stripes.

In the distance a garbled yodel came across the ice. "O-owaowa-wa-wa." A flock of birds burst from the water in a flurry of motion and settled back down. The only image of this silhouetted duck was a long thin tail that trailed behind like a giant stinger, and then that garbled song started up again. I had just seen a flock of old squaws, summer residents of the Arctic Circle who consider the Great Lakes a southern holiday.

Behind the beach dunes I skied south in open, rolling sand country, with sumac and dogwood coloring the white with their red berries and red branches. Here jackpine, oak, and birch stabilized the dunes; but the forest was young, for the sands still surged and moved in the wind. The snow was soft. It fell from the sky in the shelter of the dunes and settled softly, not wind-driven.

I turned north to enter a cathedral-like area of hemlock and white pine branches. Among the pines were yellow birch laden with seed catkins and redpolls that were busily eating the seeds. Blue jays scolded with that harsh yell that warned all others of my presence, and a red squirrel paused on a branch to echo his dissatisfaction with my intrusion.

Tracks in the snow showed where a deer had bounded down the steep dune and trotted across the trail. Deep pocks in the snow, three feet long and eighteen inches across, marked each bound. The impact of legs and body plunging into the fluff and exploding out left little detail; but the pattern of cavities four to ten feet apart showed the speed the animal had been traveling, and the formation of the snow that was showered from the spot showed which direction he had gone.

In the valley the tracks revealed the deer's two enlarged toe pads and dew claws. Less hurried here, the deer had walked slowly along the ski trail, munching on an occasional dogwood branch, leaving ragged edges of inner bark to reflect the winter light. Then the deer had moved off the trail and over a neighboring dune — and I skied on.

A chickadee sang a cheery spring song; the mood was light. Ernest Thompson Seton said that chickadees begin their spring song in February to make other birds think that they were smart to stay all winter while the others had wasted their time by going south. A blue jay chimed in with his bell notes — a light airy song that didn't seem that it should belong to a raucous jay.

I skied up over a dune for another vista and enjoyed the warmth of the sun on my face. Small tracks of a four-footed animal with a tail drag caught my eye. The tracks indicated that the animal was hopping from spot to spot, for only a line from the tail broke the snow between each set of footprints. Suddenly, from behind a tree a small deer mouse leaped out and hopped across the trail.

It looked like a miniature kangaroo as it moved, lightly placing its front feet down at each landing. Perhaps this was the image that gave Kangaroo Lake its name.

North of Sevastopol at Cave Point the winter images changed drastically. Rock-formed steps, cliffs, and sea caves gave the waters of Lake Michigan their greatest ice sculpture diversity. In the topless cave which gives the Point its name, the water had surged in and boiled up against the walls, sending great waves to slap against the rock and fill the air with fine mists to gather in the cracks. The sun's rays melted the ice on the south face; and rivulets of meltwater became suspended in long, thin, icy sabres below the sun's reach. On the north face the winter's ice buildup was unimpeded by the sun, and a thick mass of sinuous iceflow lined the wall.

The bay was covered by a solid sheet of ice when I arrived, but a south wind caused the icy cover to rise on swells and slide over the ice foot near the shore. The sheet was wind- and wave-driven, and the crush of ice filled the air with gnashing and grinding.

North of the Point the ice moved almost parallel to the shore and caught on ridges and ramparts of earlier ice movements. The immovable shoreline and the irrepressible ice mass met, and the ice buckled to form more ridges. As these ridges built up, the ice sheets surged forward, cracked, and dropped over the crest or slid back — rejects to be deposited elsewhere by the relentless conveyor.

The air was filled with crisp sounds, and the eye was kept in constant movement. The lifeless ice was more animate than any life form.

I skied the trails and had an opportunity to experience the trees of The Ridges. In this small area can be found all of the conifers of

Wisconsin, except the jackpine. On a winter's day in bright sunlight you can look at a line of evergreens and see a variety of hues that would challenge any artist's palette — from the very dark spruce to the yellowish tinge of cedar scales.

I watched white-tailed deer use these cedars as a curtain to slip away unseen. Their tracks, their droppings, and the craters where they had slept told many tales of their life.

The deer inspired me to look for wildlife, so I donned a pair of snowshoes and followed the stream from Moonlight Bay into Mud Lake Refuge. Along one bank were the prints of an otter, not the slide we associate with its winter frolic, but a deliberate walk. Further on, I found the tracks of three coyotes. The coyote trail is straight, less meandering than a dog's and slightly larger than a fox's track. Where tufts of grass made mounds of snow, yellow stains showed that they had paused to urinate, to leave that scent that informs the dog world that they were there; the territory was already claimed.

Upstream a white-tailed deer trail crossed and led toward an open spring. The spring was one of two streams that entered from the east above a beaver dam. The dam was built of ash, spruce, birch, and aspen; these feeder streams kept the reservoir well supplied with water. Along one bank stood a beaver lodge, a mound of snow with assorted sticks protruding. The sticks were ridged with teethmarks, and on top one log was light-colored and fresh-looking, an indication that the beaver had added to the lodge in the fall and was still using it. Food was scarce by this cedar- and spruce-lined stream, but this flat-tailed hermit was still surviving. I considered the sparse number of streams in the Door and felt that any beaver was a rare find.

I left the lake and retraced my way toward the road. On the opposite bank I discovered a mink track and near the stream mouth was a red squirrel path. There was little evidence of human beings in the area.

At Newport State Park I skied the shoreline to Spider Island across the packed snow of the points and through the fluff of the protected bays, then followed the trail north through beech, aspen, maple, birch, and hemlock. A pileated woodpecker led me from one bend to the next. I heard its call echoing through the woods like laughter and listened to the slow, steady, loud drumming sound as it pounded a tree trunk.

After the pileated left me and entrusted the guidework to a much smaller downy woodpecker, I reached Europe Bay, which was named for a vessel called "Europe" that sank there. In the bay is Gravel Island, a gull nesting rock in summer and an ice sculpture that breaks the blue horizon in winter.

I was skiing from Lynd Point and watching the bay rather than the woods, a habit that is hard to break along such a magnificent coast. If the porcupine hadn't scolded me with his clucking call, I might never have seen him at all. But then this was no ordinary porky. With his tail — flat and broad like a beaver's but spiked like a cactus — dangling from the branch, he was chewing his lunch. He munched steadily until, tiring of his audience, he turned and walked along the branch toward the trunk of the tree. Rather than walking directly onto the trunk, the porcupine then turned and backed off the smaller branch. I had never seen one do this, but "backing off" is probably a protective measure, as his greatest threat would come from the direction of the tree trunk and not the air. A pincushion with all the points pushing out would not be a welcome sight to a hungry carnivore.

At the trunk the porky rolled back and reached for the trunk with his forearm. In moving through the branches the porky was slow, but quite agile. He climbed a few feet to a crotch in the tree where snow had collected from the previous night's storm, hesitated, looked to see whether he was being chased, and, satisfied that he wasn't, plunged his head dreamily into the snow and ate and sipped until the snow and his thirst were gone. He climbed to another branch and sat back on his haunches with his forearms folded across his chest. It appeared that he would be the spectator now, and I left.

On the north end of the peninsula the ferry still runs between Northport and Washington Island. Ice forms along the margin of Green Bay, leaving the peninsula tip and the chain of islands that extends northeast from it half surrounded by water and half by ice. The lands are connected like a great Indian choker of rock and ice.

During the winter the ferry runs once each way each day and is forced to halt services an average of five or six days each year. Ice covered the channel between Detroit and Plum Islands, and the ferry surged forward onto the ice, crushing it beneath its weight.

On board, Ben Johnson, a retired fisherman, reminisced about his days on the lake. He told of riding the ferry for eight hours from Washington Island only to be turned back two boat-lengths from the dock by immovable ice. He also talked longingly about the 41 mile stretch he had fished between Washington and Manitou Islands. Now he and his wife were retired and enjoyed the community social life, which Mrs. Johnson said was busiest when the tourists weren't around.

Winter life can be demanding here. The next day I watched three trawlers knock the snow off their gunwales and break ice as they left the bay. Snow whipped across the farm fields of the central island, and farm horses took shelter behind wooden barns.

A wood-shingled two-story house overlooked the bay towards Detroit Island. Snow piled up in chest-high drifts along one side. In another corner two old square-logged barns stood in disarray. The wind spiraled through the glassless windows and between the logs where chinking had fallen away. Those barns looked cold but defiant, and stirred images of pioneer struggles in my imagination.

In 1856, the bitter winter closed shipping lanes, and the island received no mail or fresh supplies for three months. In 1893, when smallpox added to the struggle of the winter survival, the January weather contained both sleet and cold. The thermometer dropped to 40 degrees below zero in February. Those log homes must have been chilly.

I wandered among the ice ramparts and watched the sunset of pink and orange beside the infamous Death's Door. Rosy shades reflected on upturned triangles of ice. The sun's rays sparkled where the wind had blown the snow off the surface of the lake. The image was straight out of Jack London and needed only the savage dog team rushing across the ice pack toward the sunset. The lake was a tundra landscape with the cliffs of the mainland looming in the distance.

Peninsula State Park has ski trails and solitude, but perhaps here the real advantage of winter is neither the lack of people nor the varied trails, but rather the chance to walk on the frozen waters of the bay and to gaze at the stoic cliffs of limestone with their suspended sea caves.

There is no rocking of the boat, no drifting ashore, nor distracting sounds of pleasure craft in winter's Eagle Bay. I stood beneath Eagle Bluff in the full light of the rising sun and studied its full details. I studied lines of cedar slung about the limestone shoulders and purple-tipped birches reaching from below. The limestone picked up the yellows of the rising sun and glowed against the stark blue winter sky.

Beneath my feet the ice belched and cracked with pains of cold and motion. Nuthatches sang their nasal one-note song beneath the cliffs while downy woodpeckers hammered steady drumbeats on the trees. Sights and sounds blended into images; the images became memories which, after all, are our only real souvenirs, the most lasting of our mementoes.

This winter exploration ended at Sturgeon Bay. Solitude and peacefulness could be found in Potawatomi State Park, yet a mile away the shore was dominated by the frantic pace of winter shipyards.

The harbor is full of ships in winter, ships that seek the Sturgeon Bay shipyards for repair and renewal. Cranes divide the skyline, boats — bigger than the city's blocks — dwarf workers, bridges, and spectators.

The shipyards are a maze of floating castles with steel-masked knights who brandish acetylene torches instead of swords. At night the bay is a profusion of Fourth of July sparklers and ordered chaos. It is the antithesis of the Door's winter. It is bustle while the woods are calm, it is technology while the hillsides are square-logged houses and stovewood barns. But it is also part of the land's human heritage. In Door County it is this blend of the cultural and the natural that makes it so special.

Door County isn't New England in Wisconsin. It isn't the world's largest Icelandic settlement. It isn't the biggest cherry producer in the world. Door County is a blend of people, land, and time that is still honest and unique.

A MESSAGE FROM THE LAND

HALLOWEEN PUMPKINS, BURNT ORANGE IN COLOR LIKE THE MAPLE LEAVES THAT FLUTTERED ABOVE THEM, APPLE TREES, BOTH GREEN AND RED, AND CARICATURED SCARECROWS, SOFT SCULPTURES OF FABRIC AND IMAGINATION, ALL DECORATED MY LAST VISIT TO DOOR COUNTY. HALLOWEEN, A CELEBRATION OF ANCIENT RELIGIONS, AN

accounting of the final harvest, had charm in these symbols of man and nature. Unlike trick or treat, these symbols are aesthetic, and appropriate to this rural landscape.

The mannequins on the swing, in the grey dampness beside the Cupola House, were symbolic of the positive energy of the present and the legacy of the past. They were alone the day that we drove past. The tourists who had filled the county on the previous weekend were dim memories, but their presence was still felt.

My notes from my first day back were not all pleasant inspirations. While I enjoyed the graceful lines and art of one floral barn painting, a garish advertisement leapt from the silo on another homestead. The charms of Door County are subtle and continue to draw people, but some choose to mask the real beauty behind billboards and placards.

New, cheap thrills, amusement parks that threaten Door County with the Wisconsin Dells syndrome, are concessions designed for people who have not tasted the true fruits of life. They are for those who must be entertained because they cannot entertain themselves. They are for people who cannot observe and absorb the beauty of nature and man.

The Clearing is still a symbol of the landscape, and the artwork in local galleries, like the Eight of Pentacles Shop, remains a product of inspiration and love for the land, but the new symbols are condos and estates, more and more motels, and more campgrounds. Crowding is being promoted rather than prevented.

When the view from one condo window is another condo, when the only view the motels offer is a river of blacktop, when Peninsula State Park becomes an island surrounded by wheeled cottages, then there will be no more reason to travel to Door County.

Without local zoning, without controls, and without a feeling for the land, all of us who enjoy this land and spend our money to be here will stay home or go someplace else, if someone doesn't say, Enough.

BIBLIOGRAPHY

Apps & Strang, Barns of Wisconsin. Madison, WI: Tamarac Press. 1977.

Banks, H. P., Evolution and Plants of the Past. Belmont, CA: Wadsworth Publishing Co., Inc. 1970.

Berry, Wendell, The Long-Legged House. New York, NY: Audubon/Ballantine Books. 1969.

Black, Goldthwait & Willman, The Wisconsin on Stage. Boulder, CO: 1973.

Bosselman, Callies, Banta, The Taking Issue. Washington, D.C.: Council on Environmental Quality. 1973.

Boyer, Dwight, Ghost Ships of the Great Lakes. New York, NY: Dodd, Mead & Company. 1968.

Crowns, Byron, Wisconsin through 5 Billion Years of Change. Wisconsin Rapids, WI: Wisconsin Earth Science Center. 1976.

Door County Chamber of Commerce, A Contemporary Look at Door County. 1975.

Eaton, Conan Bryant, Rock Island. Sturgeon Bay, WI: Bayprint, Inc. 1971.

Eaton, Conan Bryant, Washington Island: 1836-1876. Sturgeon Bay, WI: Bayprint, Inc. 1972.

Eaton, Conan Bryant, Death's Door. Sturgeon Bay, WI: Bayprint, Inc. 1974.

Frost, Robert, Robert Frost's Poems. New York, NY: Washington Square Press/Pocket Books. 1971.

Fulkerson & Carson, The Story of The Clearing. Chicago, IL: Coach House Press. 1972.

Furnas, J. C., The Americans. New York, NY: Putnam's Sons. 1969.

Hole, Francis, Soils of Wisconsin. Madison, WI: U. of Wisconsin Press. 1976.

Johnston, Basil, Ojibway Heritage. New York, NY: Columbia University Press. 1976.

Josephy, Alvin M., Indians. New York, NY: American Heritage Publishing, Simon & Schuster. 1961.

Josephy, Alvin M., The Indian Heritage of America. New York, NY: Bantam Books. 1968.

Kehlart & Quinlan, Early Door County Buildings. Bailey's Harbor, WI: Meadow Lane Publishers. 1976.

King, Philip, The Evolution of North America. Princeton, NJ: Princeton University Press. 1977.

Koubs, Theodore, Wisconsin's Amazing Woods. Madison, WI: Wisconsin House, Ltd. 1973.

Martin, Lawrence, The Physical Geography of Wisconsin. Madison, WI: U. of Wisconsin Press. 1971.

Mason, Ronald, Two Stratified Sites on the Door Peninsula of Wisconsin. Ann Arbor, MI: U. of Michigan Press. 1966.

Nesbit, Robert, <u>Wisconsin History.</u> Madison, WI: U. of Wisconsin Press. 1973.

Oakley & Muir-Wood, <u>The Succession of Life Through Geological Time.</u> Portsmouth, England: Trustees of the British Museum. 1967.

Ratigan, William, <u>Great Lakes Shipwrecks and Survivals.</u> Grand Rapids, MI: Eerdmans Publishing Company. 1977.

Schultz, Gwen, <u>Ice Age Lost.</u> Garden City, NY: Anchor Press/Doubleday.

Skadden, Bill, <u>The Geology of Door County.</u> Sturgeon Bay, WI: Golden Glow Publishing. 1978.

Sloane, Eric, <u>Our Vanishing Landscape.</u> New York, NY: Ballantine Books. 1955.

Sloane, Eric, <u>Diary of an Early American Boy.</u> New York, NY: Ballantine Books. 1962.

Sloane, Eric, <u>A Museum of Early American Tools.</u> New York, NY: Ballantine Books. 1964.

Sloane, Eric, <u>A Reverence for Wood.</u> New York, NY: Ballantine Books. 1965.

Sloane, Eric, <u>An Age of Barns.</u> New York, NY: Ballantine Books. 1967.

Spinar & Burian, <u>Life Before Man.</u> New York, NY: American Heritage Press. 1972.

Telfer, Sid, Jr., <u>The Jens Jensen I Knew.</u> Ellison Bay, WI: Driftwood Farms Press. 1982.

Vander Worth, W. C., <u>Indian Oratory.</u> New York, NY: Ballantine Books. 1971.

Warren, William, <u>History of the Ojibway Nation.</u> Minneapolis, MN: Ross & Haines, Inc. 1974.